BORN ON
THE BAYOU

A Memoir

BORN ON THE BAYOU

A Memoir

BLAINE LOURD

G

Gallery Books

New York   London   Toronto   Sydney   New Delhi

AUTHOR'S NOTE

This work is a memoir. It reflects my present recollections of my experiences over a period of years. Certain names and identifying characteristics have been changed, certain individuals and events are composites, and some others are my own creations. While I have taken literary license in the telling of my story (I am a Southern boy, after all), I believe it captures the essence of my childhood and coming of age.

Gallery Books
An Imprint of Simon & Schuster, Inc.
1230 Avenue of the Americas
New York, NY 10020

First Gallery Books hardcover edition August 2015

GALLERY BOOKS and colophon are registered trademarks
of Simon & Schuster, Inc.

For information about special discounts for bulk purchases, please contact Simon & Schuster Special Sales at 1-866-506-1949 or business@simonandschuster.com.

The Simon & Schuster Speakers Bureau can bring authors to your live event. For more information or to book an event, contact the Simon & Schuster Speakers Bureau at 1-866-248-3049 or visit our website at www.simonspeakers.com.

Interior design by Robert E. Ettlin
Cover design by John Vairo Jr.
Whiskey flask in the back pocket of jeans © Steve Outram/Photographer's Choice/ Getty Images
Old cracked leather © f1 1photo/Shutterstock
Leather tag on jeans © Furtseff/Shutterstock

Manufactured in the United States of America

10 9 8 7 6 5 4 3 2 1

Library of Congress Cataloging-in-Publication Data is on file.

ISBN 978-1-4767-7385-8
ISBN 978-1-4767-7387-2 (ebook)

To Crystal, my wife, who is joie de vivre personified, and to my three sons, Brice, Cole, and Boone—I love watching you play.

I ought to go upright and vital,
and speak the rude truth in all ways.

—*Ralph Waldo Emerson*

BORN ON THE BAYOU

A Memoir

PROLOGUE

"I love New Orleans" is how most people respond when they hear that I'm from Louisiana. The truth is that New Orleans was the only thing President Thomas Jefferson really wanted in the Louisiana Purchase, but oftentimes in life, luck and being in the right place at the right time are everything.

New Orleans certainly has a rich history as a seaport, cultural center, and entertainment destination, but there is an another entire part of the Pelican State that is much more rural and exotic, and to get out of New Orleans to the other parts of Louisiana is to get into a place that is like no other, with a people like no other.

To reach these cities and small towns, you drive west over the Atchafalaya Basin, the largest freshwater swamp in the world. The Basin, as everyone in Louisiana calls it, encompasses over 1.4 million acres from the top of the state, which borders Arkansas, to the westernmost area of the state, which borders Texas, all the way to the mouth of the Mississippi River.

The lowest part of Louisiana is arguably the wettest, wildest, and freest part of the country, with over three hundred different species of birds, fifty different species of mammals, and dozens and dozens of species of reptiles and amphibians. In the heart of this spooky maze of bottomland—filled with pine trees, live oaks draped with Spanish moss, small water passes, marshes, and bayous—is New Iberia, and that's where I'm from.

New Iberia is in the heart of Cajun country. Its Main Street has not changed much since the 1800s. If you travel east on that street from the antebellum landmark Shadows on the Teche, which borders the bayou, you will find small shops, lawyers' offices, and an old gambling hall, which used to post prizefights and now posts old men playing dominoes. Moving south over an old drawbridge, you'll pass a nursing home that used to be the main hospital, and even farther south, you'll be led to old Loreauville Road, and then the old-money homes that border the main waterway, the Teche. On one side street you might see an old abandoned bait-and-tackle shop, an elementary school, and a baseball field, followed by rows and rows of cane.

Ten minutes or so from there, crossing water many times and passing the oldest sugar mill in the parish, you'll find Bluehaven Drive. Down that blacktop, all the way to the end, there stands a wood-and-brick home with large, slanting roofs, and a red brick chimney with brown and green treetops towering high above it, hiding more water behind them.

Back in 1973, when my family first moved into it, Bluehaven was in an area of Iberia Parish that the townspeople called "the country." Our lot sat at the end of a quarter-mile road that ran parallel to the bayou and was lined with large oak and cypress trees. It was rumored that the farmer who owned the land would sell off a few pieces here and again to pay off old gambling debts. For a long time, the road we lived on was dirt, grass, rock, and gravel, and while driving home at night, we used to see the glaring eyes of rabbits, opossums, and raccoons staring back at us from the rain ditches. The front yard of the house had large spans of Bermuda grass and a gigantic magnolia tree that blossomed broadly every spring. The deep side yard of the home had a small citrus grove that, for many years, the patriarch of this family tended to with great pride.

Mostly when I think about that place now, I think of him, standing in our garage among his lawnmowers and hunting decoys, a Miller High Life in his hand. In those days he hadn't hit it big yet, but if he could've bet on his chances, he'd have been all in.

1

My father was a salesman. Throngs of high school graduates, liberal arts majors, frat boys, and C students become salesmen. Others, like Dad, become *unofficially* designated as such. It is the fallback position. Born of great confidence. My father's favorite line when I was a boy was "I never had a bad day." For most of my childhood, I believed that.

In the late fifties, an affable college dropout like Dad had several choices for work in south Louisiana. He could become a sugarcane farmer, work for the Wildlife and Fisheries Department like his father, or go into oil. Dad chose the oil business—he wanted to tie his star to growth, and growth in south Louisiana meant oil.

My father was a betting man, like his father before him. But salesmen are made, not born. No one likes rejection. So there is a considerable premium to be earned for having to listen all day long to lines like "How'd you get my number, boy? I'd like to come down to that high-rise office of yours, pull off your head, and shit down your neck." Rejection pays. Always has. Always will. A salesman who takes rejection well can make money. My father was a *great* salesman.

The oil business in the South translates into "awl bidness." In 1972, when I was ten, before the oil embargo, oil was a good business. After price controls were instituted by Nixon in 1973, it was a great business. Oilmen are not dumb. Price controls prevented oil companies from passing on to consumers the rising cost of crude imports. Swifter than the politicians, they saw an opportunity. So when price controls were instituted, oil companies reduced imports and cut gasoline sales to independent gas stations in order to keep their own branded outlets supplied. The lines and shortages that form our collective memory of the oil crisis were the result of price controls—not, as is popular belief, the Arab oil embargo.

During the following years, Congress instituted a number of measures to "remedy" the situation, but they all had one thing in common, just as they always do. They distorted the market and created perverse incentives—in this case, incentives that made America more reliant on foreign crude. It's like skating to where the puck *was*; politicians and money managers do it all the time.

However, at the time, the oil embargo meant great business for the Southern oil and gas states. Though the embargo caused misery for the rest of the country, from the mid-seventies through the early eighties, there was no business better than the awl bidness. Dad had people working for him making $100,000 a year whose wives would not allow them to manage their own checking accounts—a level of wealth as disproportionate to merit in the oil business as it is cyclically known to be on Wall Street. These realities would shape our family profoundly, but not until later.

My father dropped out of college in 1959, a few years after he met Mom, a shy churchgoing blonde from Texas named Sherion. She was in awe of him. He would go to her house after school and lie on the couch while she pored over her homework. She thought he was so smart because he never had to study.

For her part, Mom had hoped to marry Dad since the day he had first winked at her in the hallway of New Iberia Senior High School. He was thin, confident, and handsome—an all-state baseball player for the New Iberia High Yellow Jackets. His eyes were so bright, they shined electric blue from his place on the dirt diamond at second base, as he kicked his cleats gently into the dirt and chattered, "Hey, batter, batter," waiting for the pitch to be thrown.

Mom's father, Clyde Burley Brice, was a six-foot-tall, soft-spoken Mason who had supported his family as a manual laborer since he had been old enough to work and too young not to cry. His friends called him C.B., and years later, I would come to know and love him as my grandfather Paw.

One of my earliest memories is of Paw walking down the long driveway of his Lietmeyer Street home after a full day at the carbon black plant, his hard hat in one hand and his gray lunch pail in the other, smiling at me as I ran up to greet him. In his prime, Paw was a towering figure to a boy of six. In his monochromatic work clothes, with his jet-black hair and wide shoulders, he looked like Johnny Cash. We would greet each other with a handshake that would quickly turn into a test of strength. No matter how old he got or how strong I got, he always won. His unchanging strength, which maintained the natural order of things, was more important to me than I could know. He'd giggle as he made me submit, and he'd always say something like "I can still whoop your butt, boy."

Paw showed me how to sharpen a pocketknife, and he taught my older brother, Bryan, how to play cards. Bryan liked playing bridge with Paw, our grandmother, Margie—whom we called Maw Brice—and Mom because, like Bryan, Paw knew how to listen.

One spring morning Paw made some over-easy eggs, crispy bacon, and biscuits, and then neatly organized the leftovers on top of the stove—to be sure to return to them later. In fact, I never saw Paw waste one morsel of food his whole life; he even went so far as to take *everything* home from restaurants in a doggy bag, down to the bones and the bread.

Even though Paw was not classically educated, he read and played various games of intellect and strategy, like bridge, chess, and gin. When we were alone with Paw, he always called us "son," and when we were all with Dad, he always called us by our names. He was a gentleman to the core.

"Son," he said to Bryan, "the key thing about bridge is, never bid too low." Bryan would listen to whatever advice Paw gave about cards, and never need clarification, because Paw was direct, and Bryan was smart. They would play bridge and gin for hours. One day when Bryan was fourteen, he confided to Paw during a bridge game that he found his opinion differing from our father's about what to do with his future.

"Son," Paw said, "Mr. Emerson said that there is a time in every man's education when he arrives at the conviction that imitation is suicide—that he must take himself, for better or for worse, as his portion." Bryan took it in, nodding in silence.

Paw had been transferred to Louisiana from Texas when he'd been promoted to manager of the Ashland carbon black plant. The only curse word he ever used was "*sheeit*," in a thick West Texas accent, and he only used it when he was out of earshot of any woman—and especially far from the hot-tempered, redheaded Margie, whom Paw always called "Wife." In turn she called him "Husband," affectionate nicknames established in an era when marriage was still considered an unshakable, lifelong, till-death-do-us-part commitment.

For most of Mom's life, Paw had not allowed her to be alone with boys, much less date them, but that all changed when they moved to New Iberia and she turned sixteen. She still had a dusk curfew, except on Friday nights, when she was allowed to stay out until eleven. She was not allowed to drive, so Margie or another church mom would pick her up and drop her off at places where other teens congregated in the late fifties, like the drive-in, the malt shop, or the American Legion baseball park—where my dad, Harvey Hopkins "Puffer" Lourd Jr., was king. My father's nickname, Puffer, was given to him by his father when he was four because he was always retrieving cigarette butts and trying to get the last puff.

Dad, for most of his teen years, had dated a girl from the neighborhood named Miriam, whose main attraction was that she lacked the Puritan morals that most of the girls in New Iberia possessed. But that changed very quickly after he was swept off of his feet by Mom's quiet beauty, angelic innocence, and rapt attention. They courted, at first, from afar at the baseball field. After a while, they talked at school, where he was a senior and she was a sophomore.

Dad's personality was infectious to behold, even then. He'd walk onto the baseball field with a swagger that said he had not a care in the world, sprinkle around a generous, confident laugh, and his teammates would spark to life in ways the coach never saw in his absence. His coach loved him, but could get frustrated with his let-the-good-times-roll attitude. "Puffer Lourd, you are a leader, son, but you are the wrong kind of leader," he'd say with concern.

There was so much glee in Dad's eyes, in the way he threw his head back in deep amusement, that whenever he told a joke, other people kind of had to laugh, even if it wasn't funny—they just wanted to laugh with him. Puff never applied himself in school, but he had a magic way of turning Ds into Cs and Cs into Bs, because teachers loved him. He was the kind of guy who, in some ways, you wouldn't want your daughter to date but, in others, you'd want him to be the only guy she ever dated. Men wanted to *be* him, and women wanted to hold him.

His skill on the baseball team was known from Baton Rouge to Lake Charles. Dad's teammates would run through a wall for him because they knew he could always be counted on to get a base hit at the right moment, and he never missed an opportunity to turn a double play. When Mom met Puffer, he had just accepted a baseball scholarship to Tulane University, where he planned to study dentistry without regard to whether or not it was a scalable profession.

One day, Mom noticed him at the local bowling alley while she was sitting with her friend Myrna at the dining counter. She was wearing a white skirt that fell below her knees, a blue sweater, bobby socks, and blue-and-white bucks—the picture of Church of Christ innocence as she sat there, her heart racing, hoping he felt the same way she did.

Across the smoke-filled room, Dad stood against a wall, a Miller High Life in one hand, a red bowling ball in the other, and a cigarette hanging from his mouth. His green-and-red–striped bowling shirt had "Puff" printed over the right front pocket and "Texaco" on the back. The hall was filled with the smell of burgers frying and the sounds of balls rolling, pins dropping, Chuck Berry on the jukebox, and men loudly talking in happy, carefree drunkenness.

Not far from the men were the young ladies, ladies of all types, sitting around the periphery of the bowling lanes—Southern women who believed their place was by a man, and had little ambition other than to marry their high school sweethearts and have children. Most were virgins. Some were pretending to be, even to their closest friends.

I can imagine my mother among them, waiting until he called out to her before she turned her head, how she must have smiled as she stared down at her Dr Pepper, her smooth, fresh face flushed with excitement. She had never been without her overbearing, judgmental mother breathing down her neck for long enough to enjoy the attentions of a boy like him. She watched him step up to the line to roll a strike with a perfect draw and then saunter away from the group of boys to say hello to his future bride.

"Hey, Sherion."

"Hey, Puff. Good game you're rolling tonight."

"Yeah, pretty good. I'm a little upset about that eight in the six frame. I was robbed. What are you doing after the game?"

"I have to be home by eleven. My dad will be waiting up for me."

"I got to come over there and get C.B. to understand that you're always safe when I'm around."

"Yeah, good luck with that."

"You doubting my sales ability?"

"No, I'm doubting my dad. But you could always come over some night and talk to him about it."

"I might just do that."

I can picture Dad there, sipping his beer through crooked lips, asking Myrna politely whether they could have a minute alone, and then looking into Mom's blue eyes.

"Did it hurt?"

"Did what hurt?"

"Did it hurt when you fell from heaven?"

That was it. She was his.

"I know we haven't known each other long. I can't explain what your smile does to me. You make me feel like settling down. Will you wear my class ring?"

"Stop it now. What about Miriam?"

"Miriam is just a friend, and she knows that a Coonass always goes his own way."

Mom was too caught up in the moment to realize the long-lasting impact that this philosophy would have on their lives. She had never met a man as dashing and handsome as Puff, with those flashing blue eyes that lit up the night.

She took his class ring right there on the spot and, later, the wedding ring he had purchased for $500 at City Jewelers on Main Street. They got married in the summer of 1959 after Mom graduated from high school, and honeymooned in New Orleans on a limited budget. She was soon pregnant with my brother, Bryan William Lourd; nineteen months after Bryan's birth came me; and fifteen months later we were joined by my little brother, Harvey Hopkins Lourd III, whom we called Tutu. I don't really know the exact definition of Irish twins, but I think we were the Cajun version—in triplicate.

I was an energetic boy, and even as an infant, I valued my personal freedom. My mother tells me there was no crib that could hold me. At five months old I would climb out of the crib and often fall on my head. By six months I could scale the side of the crib, and by the time I was one, I would vault off the side rails of the crib and hit the ground running. Oftentimes, I would hurtle out in the middle of the night, and she'd catch me at the back door of the house trying to "escape."

"Where are you going, Blaine . . . ?" she would ask as she picked me up in her nightgown. "Out . . ." I would mumble in baby-speak. She'd walk me back to the room, put me back in the crib, and I would scream for a while until she patted me to sleep.

Bryan, from the time he could talk, had responsibility. Mom and Dad treated him like an adult very early on because he was mature and could be trusted. He generally apprehended the rights and rules in a situation and made things work. When Mom had to go out to run errands and her mother, Maw Brice, wasn't around, we all went with her—Bryan was second in command. Whenever we went to the grocery store on Trotter Street, Deborah, who came along five years after Tutu, would be on Mom's right hip; Tutu would be snapped into the grocery cart, and Bryan would be holding my hand tightly so I couldn't run away.

My older brother had his hands full with me as I had a penchant for being in the wrong place at the wrong time. I had personality, because when you are the second of four, you have to find ways to be seen and heard, even if, in the end, you got your butt spanked for it. I got my butt spanked a lot.

Bryan, on the other hand, was observant and measured in his movements and actions. As the first son, the big brother, his maturation from infant to little man was quick, and over time his responsibilities grew. In fact, by the time he was thirty, he just about fully supported everyone in my family but me.

Tutu didn't talk at all until he was three, and to this day is laconic. Harvey H. Lourd III got the nickname Tutu because he and I would sit in front of the television watching cartoons, and there was this one cartoon called "Touché Turtle," about a turtle with brown legs, a green shell, and a bald head. Tutu was bald until he was five years old, and I thought he looked like Touché, so I'd point at the TV, then point at him and say, "Tuuuuuuuuu." And it stuck.

In addition to being bald and blond, Tutu was smaller than me. He had a discerning palate and would eat only pasta and sugar until he was in his teens. Despite this fact, he was rangy and thin. By the time he was twelve every tooth in his mouth had a filling in it. He liked Icees and peanut M&M's like a Viking craves grog and roasted meats, and he'd eat and drink them at will without concern for his quarterly trips to the dentist, which sometimes took two to three hours.

Tutu wasn't much into hunting and fishing, but he and Dad shared a love of baseball, and were both pretty good at it. Often after work in the mid- to late seventies, Dad would park his Lincoln behind the center field fence at American Legion, where Tutu practiced. Quietly he'd get out, hop onto the hood, and rest his back on the windshield; then he'd crack open a cold one and watch. Dad loved the ballpark—coaches hitting infield, outfielders taking fly balls, bats cracking and leather gloves popping as players kicked up dirt. After a few beers, Dad would get restless, like men do, and drive off; sometimes Tu would see him, and sometimes he wouldn't. Baseball is said to be the "thinking man's sport," which is probably why Tutu was good at it—he was a thinker. He was consistently the best math student in his class, and frugal with his words. In fact, he rarely spoke at all unless he had to.

I always looked very different from my brothers. I was just bigger, despite the fact that I was allergic to corn products and, hence, could never eat sweets. From the time he was six years old and I was four, I remained the same size as Bryan, who, like Tutu, was blond and lean. Our family diet was regular: Mondays Mom would cook pinto beans, on Tuesdays we'd have all-you-can-eat Pizza Hut, on Wednesdays it was pinto beans again, and on Thursdays, Hamburger Helper. Fridays were our big night out, and usually we'd eat crawfish or shrimp po'boys, or Dad would take us to Duck's Drive-In for cheeseburgers, malts, and fries.

And for a long time, it was as simple as that.

2

Dad's first job was as a driver and then a night dispatcher for a trucking company. He liked working nights because being off during the days allowed him to go fishing and hunting with his two best friends from high school, Fritzie and Animal. In those days, when the three of them weren't hunting, usually because the season was closed, they played sports, starting with bowling on Wednesday nights. Dad was always one of the best bowlers in the league, and even rolled a perfect game once—but baseball was closer to his heart.

Throughout the early years of their marriage, Puffer was still the fine athlete Mom fell in love with, and his softball games on the weekends were a family affair. The rec league teams mostly consisted of blue-collar workers from the oil and chemical industries—men who considered a paycheck, weekends off, and the promise of retirement at age fifty-five good enough compensation—but there was one team of lawyers who called themselves the "ambulance chasers." Dad played on his slim-pickings trucking company team, and Fritzie and Animal played for Dow Chemical and the Morton Salt company. Every Sunday after church, Mom and my siblings and I would rush to meet Dad at his game.

One Sunday in particular, after we kids had finished the usual two-and-a-half-hour Church of Christ marathon session with Mom and Paw and Maw Brice, we pulled up to the New Iberia City Park in our family's only car. It was an early-model blue-on-blue Dodge VIP Dad had purchased sight unseen from a friend of a friend in New Orleans; it'd been like new when we'd got it except for the faint scent of cherry tobacco embedded in the velour seats.

As we drove into the parking lot, I leaned against the tinted window and thought I saw Dad walking up to the batter's box, his Louisville Slugger on his shoulders. Dad was a simple man, with simple tastes, and throughout his entire life I never really did see him get attached to much, but boy, did he love that bat. He'd been using it for over a decade; it was the reliable piece of wood he'd wielded to win the Hitters Trophy in the American Legion league at the pinnacle of his baseball career. Tutu was only seven, but he was observant and had eyes like a hawk; even from the unpopular middle seat, he confirmed my sighting, screaming, "There's Dad! He's coming up to bat—stop the car, Mom!"

Excitement flickered across Mom's face as she rolled the car to a semistop, grinding the gearshift into park. Bryan, Tutu, and I hopped out, banging the long, heavy doors of the VIP shut, and ran as fast as we could in our Sunday best toward the field. As he sprinted, Tutu pulled up the back of his semiloose pants, which had once been mine, and I tried not to trip in my penny loafers; Mom always bought our shoes a half size too big to make them last longer.

Mom got out of the car quickly, and followed behind us with her purse and baby bag bouncing on one hip and Deb on the other. The three of us boys clanged against the first base fence almost in unison, our arms over our heads, fingers looped into the fence holes, as Dad spotted us and threw us that big crooked smile, pulling up just shy of the batter's box. He had on a Boston Red Sox cap, which had been purchased by his father, Hop, at the Boston train station before he took the long journey back from a weekend of horse races at Suffolk Downs. Hop, or Harvey H. Lourd Sr., was wily, a direct descendant of the earliest pioneers who developed New Iberia, and loved the ponies.

Dad always wore the number 8, in deference to his idol, the future Hall of Fame outfielder Carl "Yaz" Yastrzemski. Yastrzemski, by the time he retired in 1983, owned virtually every hitting and fielding record, not only for the Boston Red Sox but for the American League, too. Dad flipped his bat up in the air, like a juggler juggling a pin, then caught it with a surgeon's precision. He banged the bat on the bottom of his left cleat, then his right. Putting it between his legs, he spit in his hands, rubbed them together fiercely, took a deep breath, and stepped one foot into the batter's box, glancing toward the pitcher. His teammate Bob, waiting on second base, began cheering him on.

"Come on, Puff—take me home, brother, just like you do from the radio room. Here I am, Puff-n-Stuff—clear the roads for me." The pitcher looked back toward Bob on second, then stepped onto the mound. "Come on, Puff, bring me on home. I'm getting thirsty out here," drawled Bob, loud enough to make the "hot shots" in the dugout laugh.

Dad smiled, too, and stepped his other foot back toward the dugout. This was a beer league, but these guys were still young, their testosterone high and their memories of glory days not yet faded; they took winning and losing very seriously.

As Dad put the bat on his shoulder, I watched the pitcher take another quick glance at Bob on second—even though the rules clearly prohibited stealing bases. The pitcher threw a high arcing pitch, and Dad watched it go by as the weekend umpire mumbled, "Ball."

The catcher throttled the ball back to the pitcher for emphasis, and Dad tapped the bat once on the outside corner of the plate, then hoisted it back up into the air. The pitcher quickly threw a high looping strike. I saw Dad's leg cock, his eyes watching the ball float all the way toward the bat as he stepped into it with a *crack*. The third baseman jumped high, but the ball sailed about two feet over his outstretched glove.

Mom screeched, "Go, Puffffff!" at the top of her lungs and hopped up and down with Deb.

Bryan, Tutu, and I screamed, "Go, Dad," too, clanging at the fence.

Bob took off quickly toward third, and the ball skipped hard, right inside the foul line, then banged into the left field corner fence—where it ricocheted as Bob rounded third. As Dad took second, he didn't even pause, just barreled on. Bob slowed, trotting the last fifteen feet to home, knowing he'd score easily, as Dad ran like a deer, finally sliding smoothly into third base. He popped up quickly and dusted off his butt and pant leg; the third baseman threw the ball to the dejected pitcher, who snapped it up curtly and walked back to the mound. Dad tipped his hat to us boys as we clapped with the crowd; then he looked directly at Mom and took a deep bow, sweeping his hat from his head down to the ground, like a matador doing a veronica after a bull has passed.

The pitcher looked at Dad, then at Mom.

"Okay, Romeo—Puff-n-Stuff—now you are starting to rub it in. Let's play ball . . ."

The next guy up to bat was one of the drivers at Dad's trucking company; I only knew him as Mr. Hank. A mountain of a man, Mr. Hank always sported a black-and-red Mack Truck hat, along with a belly he'd been working on for years. He took a big swing at the first pitch and hit it to the fence, deep into right field, where the fielder caught it with only about a foot to spare. Dad tagged up third base and jogged in to score a run. After he crossed the plate, he walked right by us at the fence, smiling.

"Morning, Momma, boys . . . and girl," he said as he grabbed the fence where Mom stood with Deb, puckered his lips, and reached his face between one of the holes. Mom moved her mouth to his, and they kissed.

"Nice hit," she offered, pulling away shyly.

"Thanks."

After their kiss, Mom lifted Deb to the fence, and Dad kissed her on the head.

I'd never seen Mom smile more proudly, or look more beautiful.

As I watched Dad step into the dugout, high-fiving and slapping hands with the other players, Mom made her way to the bleachers, sitting down between two or three of the other wives—all of whom had big hair, were modestly well dressed, and donned baby bags and purses much like Mom's.

"Hey, Sherion."

"Hey, Tammy Lynn."

"Boy, that man of yours is lighting 'em up today. I think he's three for three, and not a ball gets by 'im."

"That's my guy . . . How's Jim doing?"

"You know, the usual—struck out once, flied out twice, took a base on balls. Caught a pop-up, which is good, I guess. Oh, and he's had at least five beers by now—but when I ask him, he'll say three." They all laughed.

As Deb got up to climb around, a little unstable in the bleachers, Bryan hopped up to hold her hand. They climbed to the top of the aluminum structure, weaving slightly, Bryan unfaltering in his anticipation of her path.

As the inning ended, Dad took his place at shortstop, and Tutu and I kicked off our penny loafers and socks, rolled them into balls, and gave them to Mom, who put them in her purse.

"Don't ruin your church clothes, boys!"

Tu and I hustled over to the third base side of the park—onto a large patch of grass and dirt, where we joined in a game of handball with some of the other kids. Tu and I always played together, and took our usual positions on the makeshift field for the underhand team in an economy that was never questioned. Tu was a fine athlete, and already making a name for himself in the ballparks straddling the bayous and cane fields of New Iberia. He was quick, agile, and smart.

"Now we gotch'y'all, Tutu's here . . ." said the pitcher of our team as he tossed the crumpled waxed paper cup to Tutu. Tu smiled humbly, took the mound, and immediately went into a long windup. He could throw sinkers, curve balls, fastballs, knuckleballs, changeups, and sliders. He was something to watch, be it wax-ball or real baseball. During the wax-ball games, I always played catcher; catchers are usually big guys. My favorite big leaguer at the time was a man named Johnny Bench—a sure-handed slugger with a big arm who played for the Cincinnati Reds, the best team in the league during the seventies.

Tu would wind up and throw strike after strike. He could throw it overhand or sidearm; it didn't matter. We'd give the younger kids five strikes to hit, and most of them still couldn't. Occasionally one of the other boys would whine or get boisterous about a call I'd made as catcher/umpire, but most of them knew they were outgunned and outmanned with Tu on the mound. Whenever they did manage to connect their hand with the wax-ball, they'd celebrate like it was Fat Tuesday on Bourbon Street—hootin' and hollerin'.

We'd play for hours, or until Dad's games ended. As the adult play-ers bagged their bats and gloves and strolled off the field to meet their families, we'd rush back to the stands and beg Mom for a few dollars for hot dogs and Cokes. Most of the time, she'd say we could have one or the other, and some of the time, we'd get nothing.

"Sorry, boys, I don't have any money."

And when she said it, we didn't complain or argue. We knew what she said was simply true—for us, and all the families at the ballpark. This was a Coonass crowd, through and through. And when I say "Coonass"—which technically relates to a certain type of Cajun—I'm not talking about a class distinction; it's richer than that. A Coonass can be wealthy or poor, wise or foolish. He can be white-collar or blue-collar. However, at heart, he's generally unpre-tentious and comfortable with himself, listens to his gut, has horse sense, and, yes, tends to be indulgent. Maybe it's the French influ-ence, or maybe it's just deep Southern roots, but Coonasses really like to have a good time. *Laissez les bon temps rouler.* Loose. Wild. Willing.

Louisianans who don't define themselves as such might say that Coonasses are lazy, dumb, or close-minded. Those less familiar with it might construe the term "Coonass" as being a slur—or, worse, something equivalent to the "N word." Then there are those Loui-sianans who would cock a smile and say that, while ornery, Coon-asses are proud, resourceful, witty, and shrewd. But if you are one, you know that being a Coonass is what you make of it—and in the end, it's an identity. Shared proudly.

And that was certainly true of this crowd of families out to have a good time with a softball or a balled-up wax cup; we didn't sweat anything that wasn't there. Occasionally we'd go with some of the other players' families to get hamburgers, but most of the time we'd go home, and Mom would cook Hamburger Helper, or we'd eat pinto beans and ham, or Dad would barbecue chicken to a true crisp. And simply enjoy it.

When Dad first started working with the trucking company, it was as a "hot shot" driver. He drove a one-ton pickup truck all over south Louisiana, delivering equipment such as drill bits, portable light plants, industrial-size water hoses, drilling chains, and all sorts of tools that drilling rigs needed in their twenty-four-hour-a-day job of searching for oil.

Drilling for oil is fraught with all sorts of challenges. Many things can go right, but many more things can go wrong when the earth's surface is punctured and pressure builds as a string of pipe goes deeper and deeper into the ground. Oftentimes, the drill bit is lost or broken off into the hole, or the overall pressure at depth is higher than the drilling engineer estimated, and they need more or less fluid; all sorts of things are needed to improvise the operation. As the increasing value of natural resources hit in the late fifties and early sixties and kick-started interest in the Southern oil patch, the entrepreneurial spirit filled the demand with all sorts of service-related businesses.

J.R. Smith Transport hot shot drivers would gather and deliver anything a tool pusher, or drilling engineer, needed to turn the drill pipe to the right—meaning dig the hole. Mr. Smith's son, J.R. Jr., played baseball with Dad in high school, and both he and his father were always fond of Puffer. As J.R.'s small business grew, he hired some of the players as cheap, part-time labor to do odd jobs for him; some of the more responsible ones, he'd hire to drive his trucks, which, at the height of the oil business, numbered more than fifty. The most responsible ones, he'd let deliver tools.

After Dad married Mom and his college years ended, he eventually took on more hours and ultimately became a full-time driver. J.R. had extreme business energy and a fine eye for opportunity. He was an early adopter of citizens band radios and, unlike most of his competition, had a radio installed in every one of his trucks. He had a large map of Louisiana in his office, stuck with thumbtacks that represented each one of his drivers, and he managed them from a company-wide public-address system so everyone knew where everyone else was. He called his office "Grand Cajun Station," and from that map and with his radio, he knew all employees' whereabouts at all times.

Sometimes, when they were really busy, Mr. Smith would work twenty-four hours a day, occasionally leaning back in the old green vinyl-wheeled chair with the varnish worn off the arms and shutting his eyes. He didn't need much sleep, though, and never, ever looked tired; he didn't have much interest in anything besides work and his Tuesday night Masonic Lodge buffet. His wife had an old army cot put in his office, but it was never used, as he always said, "The chair is just more comfortable."

Mr. Smith paid time and a half to guys who'd drive at night, and since Dad's first priority was hunting and fishing, he'd often volunteer for "on call" work. Dad loved the solitude that driving provided, and loved talking on the CB radio. He'd drive the dark roads of the Pelican State and tell other drivers stories or teach them jokes. They all loved Dad, and they'd listen for hours. Mr. Smith and his two secretaries, Tammy and Debbie, would take the incoming calls and position the drivers based on the "order flow," but every time Mr. Smith got a chance to listen to Dad tell stories, he'd lean back in his chair and smile.

Dad had what the Spanish call duende. Duende is hard to explain, but you know it when you see it, and in short, it is an ability to connect with people at all levels deeply. It is charisma, in the extreme. You don't learn duende in school; the Spanish say it comes from a higher power. Even though Dad was a few semesters shy of a degree, he was smart—certainly smarter and better educated than the rest of the drivers who worked for J.R. Smith—and Mr. Smith knew it.

One night while returning from a long trip to and from Beaumont, Texas, Dad walked into the office, and Mr. Smith called out, "Harvey, is that you?"

"Yes, sir, Mr. Smith, it's me," Dad said, simultaneously humming the Jerry Lee Lewis blues tune "Big Legged Woman" and wondering how the hell J.R. always could tell a person by the way the door shut.

"One day you are going to tell me how you do that."

"It's called calculus, son; I can tell you where every one of our drivers are right now based on the time they left here, the time they picked up or dropped off the load, and length of the roads they traveled back. Not to mention your chatter on the airwaves."

"I haven't said a word in hours. Seriously, Mr. Smith . . . that's a talent. You missed your calling; you should've been an astronaut, or something."

"I like money too much," he replied humbly, adding, "Speaking of a calling, Harvey, what do you want to do with yourself?"

"What do you mean, Mr. Smith?"

"Son, you are way too smart to drive a truck for the rest of your life, and pardon me for noticing, but that wife of yours is way too pretty to be fed only ducks, geese, dove, and Basin deer."

"Yes, sir, she is pretty, and it don't hurt to look . . ."

"Mrs. Smith never learnt that little fact." He chuckled. "Anyway,

Harvey, I was thinking you should come into the office, handle the PA system when I'm not, and you could help J.R. Jr. run the office, too."

"So, Mr. Smith, are you telling me you'd pay me more to sit in here in the air-conditioning, and I wouldn't have to drive drill bits to Beaumont?"

"Yes, I am."

"Hmm." Dad looked down at his worn-out steel-toe work boots. "Lemme ask you this, Mr. Smith—could I work some nights during hunting season?"

"Yeah, I'm sure the night dispatcher wouldn't mind, and you could take a shift or two of mine. We could work that out."

Dad smiled. "Sounds good. I'll do it."

"Aren't you going to ask me how much more money you'll make?"

"Mr. Smith, I know you'll take care of me, you always have, and anyway . . . more is more. And if I get to hunt on Wednesdays, we are good."

"Okay, Harvey. We'll start next week."

J.R. Smith's transport office sat on about three acres of graveled parking lot, on a little side road right off the St. Martinville highway, near one of the sugarcane mills. The dispatching area and Mr. Smith's office were in the back of the building, and their windows faced about twenty-five acres of wooded bottomland that Mr. Smith's father had left him. Dad loved his new position, but he especially loved the night shift. All alone—just him, a microphone, a captive audience of Coonass truck drivers, and a large window that faced out into the beauty of the sportsman's paradise.

At dusk, he'd talk to drivers, lean back in his stretched-out chair, and watch the wood ducks and birds dart in and out of their roosts, and when the evenings were cool, he'd let the night air filter in through the open door. Puff kept watch at a small desk, that serene view surrounding him, intermittently checking his wall-mounted US Geological Survey map of the state of Louisiana, with his receiver button pressed down.

"Listen up, night-timers, this is Puff-n-Stuff, your sweet-talking brother for the evening. I'll be your guiding light till sunup, so keep your ears open and your eyes on the blacktop, 'cause Puffer's gonna bring you home to Momma nice and easy."

Dad loved Mr. Smith, and loved his schedule, but J.R. Jr. was the heir apparent. Blood is always thicker than water, and soon, with a couple of kids to feed and more groceries to buy, Dad had to look for a better way to make a living. Mr. Smith took Dad's news of moving on seriously, though, being as he was a master Freemason.

Freemasonry is essentially a fraternity that observes a system of morality based in allegory, as put forth by old-world symbols—the medieval tools of the square and compass—which speak to man's cycle of being born, living, and dying. They are meant to remind Masons that every story remains the same, and that while on earth, the only thing that matters is service to mankind and love of your brothers. Mr. Smith had been attending meetings most of his life, and by now just lived it—so when Dad explained his conundrum, he got him a job as an apprentice surveyor at the Texaco oil company. And boy, was that good.

Texaco was the big time in New Iberia. They had a scaled-up business with multiple layers of management and job opportunities of every type, all the way up the ladder. Dad was promoted to land-man and surveyor quickly—as all he had to do was talk to farmers about drilling rights and mark off property lines.

In this new incarnation, Dad had joined the corporate world and worked in Texaco's four-story building on Jane Street. Every day he wore a white, short-sleeve, button-down shirt with a black or blue skinny tie and gray pants. He sported horn-rim glasses and carried a mechanical pencil and a pen in his pocket. His fluorescently lit office had vinyl floors and no windows, and while office bound, he'd sit in a cheap industrial chair at a metal desk with a small lamp, his surveying maps tacked up across the walls in front of him, along with his one framed picture of the three of us boys and Mom from a birthday party. After a few years, he got a white company car and a five percent yearly raise, until he was making $1,200 a month at Texaco. My best friend, Cecil Jr., thought Dad worked in a gas station. My brother, Bryan, was convinced that he was in the Coonass mafia. I just thought he had it made.

3

My sister, Deborah Kay Lourd, was born in 1968, a full five years after Tutu. Waiting for her birth, we boys drove around Dauterive Hospital on Duperier Street in the backseat of my dad's 1966 Olds 88—Bryan on my left and Tutu beside him—while Dad smoked menthol cigarettes and sipped Miller Lite, treating us to Cherry Coke Icees from the Stop & Shop on Trotter Street. At that point in Louisiana very few husbands sat in the delivery room with cameras and ice chips. It was the end of summer, but it was still very hot and humid. Dad hummed along with the AM radio with Bryan leaning over his shoulder, asking him questions about Mom and our future sister. Puff answered Bryan's questions patiently as Tutu and I looked out the windows at the boys playing basketball and riding bicycles on the streets.

Mom had always wanted a girl, as most mothers do, and by luck or accident, it finally happened. It's still not clear where "Deborah" came from, but "Kay" was my mother's middle name. She had a mane of beautiful red hair, blue eyes, and ultimately a magnificent laugh. Mom welcomed her as all moms do—excited, loving, relieved she was healthy, and expectant that she'd eventually get to do things that moms can only do with girls: play dress-up, buy makeup, talk about boys, and eventually, of course, help her choose a wedding dress. Dad, on the other hand, was just trying to provide as best he could, and adjusted very little when it came to parenting a daughter.

Dad stopped working for Texaco in 1973, and went to work at Atchafalaya Workover in Lafayette. The president of the company was a petroleum engineer named David Williams, a graduate of Texas A&M University—an Aggie. I liked "Big Dave." He was a large man with a large personality. He owned a forty-three-foot Hatteras fishing yacht moored at Grand Isle that I could not wait to go aboard. Dad said that Big Dave was the best salesman ever to enter the oil business; however, he liked to play more than he liked to work, and he had a reputation for negotiating past good faith.

To celebrate Dad's move to Atchafalaya Workover, Big Dave threw a barbecue at the prefab building that housed his executive offices and machine shop. As our family entered the party, we walked with our chests out, feeling bullish, drafting off of Dad's breakout moment of optimism.

"Use your manners," Dad reminded us calmly but sternly, so I pulled and stretched my number 33 purple-and-gold jersey away from my stomach. Bryan, his hair swept cleanly to the side, already wearing his clothes neatly, did nothing, and despite his slightly skewed look, Tutu chose not to alter his clothing either, while Deb pulled absently at her pigtails. As we pushed forward, I noticed smoke wafting out of the two oil-drum steel pits and a black man in an all-in-one jumpsuit basting roasting meats with a thick brown sauce. My mouth watered. I could hear glasses clinking, muddled laughter, and a Cajun fiddle and guitar jangling from outdoor speakers. I felt the nervous excitement I always sensed when meeting important new people.

Ms. Caroline, Dave's wife, met us near the large pull-down aluminum door—she looked like a beautiful Roman matron, her bosom shaking as she pranced out to meet us, her hair down to the base of her ass, wearing the smile of a salesman's wife.

"You must be Sherion," she said, reaching for my mom and hugging her. Mom flashed a smile and gave her the obligatory hug, pretending they were friends. Dad kissed her cheek—something I had never seen him do to any woman other than Mom or my grandmothers—and then she eyed all of us up and down, the diamonds on her hands and neck flashing in the sun.

"My, what a good-looking group of young people," she said, then pointed at me and declared, "And oh my, no doubt who you belong to—you look just like your daddy." I'd heard this many times before, and it always made me feel good. "Y'all come on in and meet the rest of the gang."

Dad and Mom stepped from the seashell-and-gravel parking lot into the spotless vinyl-floored machine shop, where not a tool was out of place; it even smelled good. The place was bigger than I'd expected, with more people than I'd ever seen at a New Iberia BBQ. We were in the city now, not country Coonass territory. Dad shook some hands as Caroline introduced him and Mom to the hoi polloi of the oil field. Most men wore western shirts and blue jeans, and the women wore pretty much the same, some in denim dresses just past the knee, but all adorned with the jewelry of the nouveau riche.

None of us had met Big Dave yet, but I knew who he was the minute I saw him. When his gaze caught ours from across the room, he quickly wrapped up his conversation and rolled our way. At about five feet ten inches tall, he sported a devilish white-toothed grin, thick curly hair, beady black eyes, and a potbelly born of living the good life.

"Harvey, this is the second happiest day of my life!" Dave said as he pumped Dad's hand, his belly shaking.

"Dave, this is Sherion, my wife," Dad said manneredly.

"Oh . . . my . . . be still my beating heart. Sherion, you are even more beautiful than he described." I had never actually seen a man flatter and almost flirt with another man's wife in front of him until this moment, but it was done with an economy and smoothness I respected. I wondered what the happiest day of his life was as he never finished the thought.

"Nice to meet you, Mr. Williams," Mom said.

"Oh no, no, no . . . you call me anything but 'Mr. Williams,' cher." ("Cher" is a Cajun term of endearment, meaning "my sweet.") "Dave, Big Dave, Lil Dave, Honey Dave—anything but Mr. Dave or Mr. Williams, please," he appealed. In all of two minutes, I realized why Dad liked Dave—why we all did. He made me happy, hopeful. It was an art he and Dad shared.

"Okay . . . Dave."

The machine shop part of the warehouse was clean, bright, and cavernous, while the executive offices were spacious, richly colored, and well appointed. There was a full kitchen, with an industrial stove, a refrigerator-freezer, a picnic table, and even a vending machine. Dave was a forward thinker in 1976. Bryan and I followed him and Dad into the offices, while Tu, Deb, and Mom meandered slightly behind us.

"And this is where your dad is going to sit for the next thirty years, I hope!" announced Big Dave as he opened the door to Dad's new office and crooned, "Voilà," in a French accent. Dad's desk was mahogany—twice the size of the old metal one he'd worked from at Texaco. He had a name placard, a large swivel chair, and pen-and-pencil set to match his leather desk blotter. The walls were adorned with drilling rig photos from the Gulf of Mexico, helicopters landing or taking off from a few of them. I read all the helipad monikers, identified as "PENROD 715," "HUNT #37 D," and the like. There was a pair of taxidermied ducks in flight beside a large, black-lacquer–framed map of Louisiana hanging behind his desk—a sense of place and purpose prevailed. Dave was proud, my parents were proud, and we all just stood there in awe as we took it all in—the American dream.

"This is it, boys and girls—your dad is gonna be a force to be reckoned with, and your life is only going to get better, and better, and better . . ." Big Dave barked. As we continued past the door marked "David M. Williams, President," he added, "My office is a mess, you guys can see it next time—let's go get some food." Later, I realized this had been Dave's way of reinforcing that this was Dad's party, not his; Dave didn't want to show up Dad in front of his kids with a bigger display of grandiosity.

At parties in Louisiana every man eventually makes it out to the cooking area and ends up peppering whoever's manning the grill or pot with comments like "Lemme take a peek at the meat," or "Lemme have a taste of the sauce," or "Hey, man, what did you use for seasoning?" or "How long did you marinate that meat?" Because every Coonass, no matter how rich or poor, how old or young, thinks he's some sort of saucier. Every Coonass has his own special grilling tools, his own special pot to cook in, and hand-me-down recipes from relatives long gone. There are few things dearer to the south Louisiana culture than food. So, as Tutu and I threw a football between some drill pipe and a mud shaker, I watched Dave, in his red all-in-one jumpsuit and black gator cowboy boots, waddle out to the BBQ pit with his newest salesman, Dad, in tow, followed closely by another man wearing well-starched Wrangler jeans. They were all respectfully hungry. Tutu overthrew me on a short wheel route, and the ball tumbled near Dave. It kicked up gravel as I jogged to it, and I overheard them talking.

"Harvey, this is Al Patout, he's our inside man at Humble

Oil . . . and a very, very important customer of ours." Dad smiled at Al, stood up a little straighter, and reached out his hand.

"Harvey, I know you . . . I was in your flight at the '74 oil-man's golf tournament at Tri-Parish. Shit, you beat my team by four strokes," Al marveled.

"Please, call me Puff. I remember you, too—big, faded drive you play," Dad asserted.

"That's him!" Dave joined in. "Although, personally, I really don't like to play that much golf; I prefer boats and indoor sports, if you know what I mean . . ." Dave said with a wink. They all laughed, as men do at innuendo, and I grabbed the ball.

"Harvey, so on every job at Humble, before submitting bids or quotes, you call Al, okay? He'll make sure our bids get 'read' right . . . and we'll make sure he gets a little lagniappe, know what I mean?" Al cocked his head a little and smiled as Dave put a hand on each man's shoulder.

Al stared at Dad until Dad's uncertainty crept into a little smile. Even though I was too young to know exactly what it was, I knew I'd just witnessed a small compromise, and that it didn't feel right. I tossed the ball deep to Tutu, and he caught it on a dead run.

Dad rode the Big Dave wave for about four years, and during that period our lives changed on every level. Dad came home with a new company car every six months or so, always a hand-me-down from Dave but certainly flashy and nice. Mom got her first new car, a light-blue Mercury Monterey with a dark vinyl top, and on the weekends our Sunday barbecues were upgraded from back-of-the-shelf pork chops to rib eyes. Dad's oil-company customers became his friends, so he saw less of Fritzie and Animal and entertained at more ostentatious, private hunting camps, golf tournaments, or fishing rodeos. Dad gifted Mom with jewelry on her birthday, their anniversary, and Christmas, and the two of them even went to a few holiday black-tie events, Dad always treating her to a new dress.

Dad learned a lot and developed a taste for success. Four years was what it took for him to feel confident enough to strike out on his own. He was making good money, but Big Dave was making great money, and Dad figured if Big Dave could do it, why couldn't he? And so the ascent began.

He left Atchafalaya Workover and, together with a man named Walter Messa, opened his own drilling consulting firm. They called it L&M Specialties, and their corporate offices consisted of two rooms in the back of a red brick building in downtown New Iberia across from Texada's Jewelry store. All the real work occurred in the field, however—these rooms were just a place to make and take calls. And it sure did make Dad happy to work for himself.

In those days Dad would rev up his 1972 purple-and-black Dodge Super Bee Charger at six a.m., as if to say, "I'm off to work, boys. Study hard." The Super Bee had dual exhausts, a 425-HP/ Hemi V8, hood locks, sixteen-inch tires with raised white letters that read "Goodyear," chrome reverse deep-dish rims, and a body-length decal that made the car seem faster than it was. I was especially impressed with the hood locks—some preadolescent automotive version of the chastity belt, I guess. Soon he traded in the Super Bee for a powder blue Lincoln Continental. Every Coonass in Louisiana wanted one. If they couldn't afford a Lincoln, they bought a Mercury Marquis instead.

From 1974 to 1984, my father spent the early part of his mornings in L&M's Main Street office with the only professional on his staff, a petroleum engineer named Ben Dugas. Dad would get to the office at six thirty a.m., about the time oilmen began making their phone calls to hire consultants. He would talk to drilling superintendents, geologists, and other people about drilling projects, pay a few bills, put out some fires, take a few orders, talk to Ben, drink coffee, and that would be it. Except for a few calls here and there, by nine a.m. every day Dad was heading down to the track to check on his prize filly. I believe it was Mark Twain who said, "A consultant is someone who can almost justify his fees."

The drilling business is a twenty-four-hour-a-day job for those on the rigs—the tool pushers, the drillers, the roughnecks, the cooks, and the roustabouts. Dad didn't get his hands dirty; he supplied goods and services. His real work was entertaining customers, mostly geologists and petroleum engineers who worked for big companies like Exxon, Shell, Mallard Well Service, McMoRan, and Texaco; he'd take them to lunch or out hunting; he'd give them tickets to Saints games, and generally try to make them feel important so that they'd in turn pass him their business.

Dad's gamble paid off. He was charismatic, and now he knew the ropes, so L&M took off. Unlike most everyone else in New Iberia, Dad had left a permanent, pensioned position to strike out on his own. Many of the naysayers, the company men, said he'd never make it, but he believed that, as Virgil stated, "Luck favors the brave."

And for a long time, that seemed true enough.

Eventually, Dad bought Walter out of the partnership but kept the *M* in the corporate name and kept his friendship with Walter. I used to ride with my dad over to Walter's and watch the two of them drink Budweiser and boil crawfish. Walter wore a pair of all-in-ones with Dad's name on them, and Dad wore a pair that belonged to some guy named Pete. They often got drunk, and that afternoon was no exception. I'm sure Dad would have preferred that I drive us home that night, but I didn't have my license yet.

Driving under the influence wasn't considered a criminal offense in Louisiana. After all, the to-go cup was invented in New Orleans and is still a popular way to wish a departing guest farewell.

As we rolled home from Walter's, we sang along with Waylon Jennings's hit "I'm a Ramblin' Man" on the radio. Waylon was one of Dad's favorites, a musical outlaw. With his long hair, black guitar, leather vest, and music so different than anything we'd heard before, Waylon was like a country biker—playing by his own set of rules. Dad, in his own way, was the same guy.

During a five-year span in the early seventies, oil prices rose 500 percent, making Dad's rise to affluence in the upper-middle ranks of the oil world meteoric. He made more money than we could spend. Oil companies hired L&M's consultants to work on their rigs at $500 a day with L&M Specialties taking 40 percent of that, pretax. In 1981, at the top of the oil boom, every day L&M had twenty consultants working on rigs in the Gulf of Mexico, south Louisiana, and parts of Texas.

Dad would call on clients all over the state with a business card in one hand and a bottle of Crown Royal in the other. The fathers would drink the Crown Royal, and the sons would save the blue felt bags with the gold drawstrings for their marijuana stashes. Dad would have enjoyed his first few beers already by the time he sidled up to his sturdy, well-clad client and affably presented a bottle. It was an invitation to shoot the shit, really, and no one was better at the follow-up than Dad. He made customers feel like his best friends, like insiders at some unspoken lottery, riding the wave without a whisper of concern, at least for the hours they sat alongside him.

Most of the affiliated salesmen drove around in white Ford LTDs with double-whip antennas, one for their dispatch radios and the other for their citizens band radios. Dad's CB handle, Puff-n-Stuff, was a combination of his nickname and the big purple cartoon dragon from Saturday morning television.

As a young boy, I liked the white company cars that cruised around south Louisiana. The back dashboards were lined with rows of colorful baseball caps embroidered with the names of all the different drilling and service companies that profited from the boom. I admired the oilmen—"oil field trash," as they were known—and I grew up taking it for granted that I would be one of them. By a certain age, every other career option was dead to me. I sketched oil rigs, fishing boats, hunting jeeps, and airplanes during math class, knowing that when I grew up I wanted to be just like them.

4

In the summertime in Louisiana, Saturdays are for grass cutting. There aren't any gardeners or landscape architects in south Louisiana. Men cut their own grass, have their sons do it, or hire a neighborhood kid for twenty bucks a tank. There are men and there are garden tools, and that's it.

Dad had a thing for lawn tools. He liked lawn mowers and weed eaters the way most men like cars. At one point during the oil-boom years, our garage on Bayou Bend Road housed three riding lawn mowers—an eight-, a ten-, and a twelve-horsepower model. I would sometimes sneak into the garage with the lights off, before Dad got home, and ride those beasts, the noonday sun peeking through cracks in the roll-up garage door. It was 1972; I was ten at the time, and wanted to know what all the gauges and knobs did, and know them by name. So I would wait for him.

Our property on Bayou Bend Road was approximately one and a half acres in size, situated across the street from a sugarcane field, and originally purchased by my father from an old whiskey runner named George Blumenthal. It was the last lot Old Man Blue still owned in the Bluehaven Drive subdivision, and the last residence we lived in before Dad's involvement in the oil boom bumped us up to a whole new kind of living. Dad was eyeing the horizon at that point, but was still working for Texaco. Saturdays there defined my childhood. They were the lull before the storm.

Around noon on these days, Dad, drunk from visiting with clients, would turn onto the gravel road and fishtail his large automobile all the way down to our house. Normally, he'd step from his car with a Miller Lite in hand, his boots freshly shined. He most always had a six-pack in a brown paper bag under his arm. He would add this fresh six-pack to the case or two already in the outside refrigerator, then change his clothes, find his favorite mower, and pull the cord. It was a good day when the engine started on the first pull. No matter, though, because if one of the mowers wouldn't start, he had two more as backup.

Dad was particularly faithful to one type of riding lawn mower, the Snapper. It was red and white and had a Briggs & Stratton engine mounted on the back. The Snapper had four mowing levels, three gears, and bicycle-like handlebars. He never liked John Deeres. I secretly suspected it was because John Deeres were too run-of-the-mill. Once Dad had an opinion, he was loyal to it.

His weed trimmers were a different story. It seemed that at least twice every summer he would come home with some new model. The garage was littered with all types of antique edging tools. There was a burnt orange one that was electric, a battery-powered one that was silver, and at least three different types that were gas powered. No matter how hard he tried to embrace the electric, he always ended up with a piston-driven machine in his hand.

At some point Dad pretty much settled on the Poulan brand. We had a Poulan chain saw and several Poulan weed trimmers. Some had two-stroke engines and some had four-. He liked the two-stroke best because they were loud and required a careful, chemist-like mixture of gas and oil.

There was a grace and finesse in his ability to distinguish and manipulate the strengths of these variegated machines. It was all trial and error, so I'd sit atop Mom's abandoned western horse saddle and watch while he tweaked, rejected, and revitalized various parts and chargers. Dad called me a soda pop cowboy.

Dad generally organized his mowing from the front yard to the backyard. The front yard was about a four-beer job. He drank the first beer while gassing up the Snapper, and then he'd open the second one after he'd climbed aboard. He would start to the right of the house near a small scrub oak and cut the grass on Mr. Blue's lot as a courtesy since Mr. Blue and Dad's father, Hop, were best friends. I liked that Mr. Blue got something out of the deal; it made Dad cooler.

He always cut the front yard in a square spiral pattern, working from the outside until all the grass was piled in the middle, careful always to point the exhaust toward the center of the yard so as not to strew blades in the driveway or the flower beds in front of the house. This is known as the Coonass raking prevention method. After completing the first section, he'd put the Snapper in neutral and walk to the yellow Frigidaire in the garage to retrieve his third beer.

About halfway through the job, he'd slam the empty can at the garbage can—or in it, if he was lucky—and then finish the front lawn, the quickest and easiest part of the job. After finishing the front, he'd get off the mower, take a piss by the oak next to the overgrown, unkempt garden, top off the gas tank, grab another beer, and move to the backyard. I knew by this point he'd greased his own wheels, too, and was starting to enjoy the sun's hot rays on his face, the rhythm in his speed. Those cold, sweating cans of confidence looked better by the minute.

The backyard of our home was level for about forty feet and then became a deep, downward-sloping, dangerous hill covered with potholes, huge pecan trees, and bush. Squirrels, robins, crows, bats, rabbits, and snakes were everywhere. I loved watching them scatter at the sound of the mower, darting or slithering deeper into the woods, as if somehow they knew Dad waited for nothing.

About seventy-five yards from the back of the house, our land met the cypress-covered banks of the Bayou Teche, a freshwater tributary about 125 miles long that flows southeast from the Atchafalaya River near Morgan City. Sugarcane growers, fishermen, and hunters, as well as oil and gas barges and field-worker transports, used the bayou. Hundreds of drainage pipes poured raw sewage into the bayou until the Clean Water Act of New Iberia was passed in 1979. At that point, we all got septic tanks. When the rains were heaviest from hurricanes or tropical storms, the water would flood the banks all the way up to the huge pecan trees, and sometimes, so would the snakes—thick-bodied, poisonous water moccasins. Seeing that fresh, glassy water running so high on the banks always made me want to go for a swim.

Dad didn't feel that way, though; he was happy gazing out at that river, shallow in some places and very deep in others, its lowlands home to many hundreds of different types of plants, birds, mammals, reptiles, and amphibians. In fact it's not uncommon to see brown pelicans perched on its banks or gliding in flocks along its edges in and out of the bald cypresses laden and moist with pale Spanish moss. At dusk, sometimes the silhouetted trees cast billowing shadows across the blankets of alligator weed that coated the surface of the waterway, creating the illusion of dry land slowly wavering and shifting through the gray-green mist and fog. You can count on Louisiana to hide things.

Taking a deep breath, Dad would start at the bottom of the hill and cut a few sections, careful not to flip the tractor near the bayou where nobody could see him. He had a deep respect for the power of nature and the limits of machines, and would push each only so far.

Dad was not prone to clearing the mower's path. He urged us, on occasion, to pick up the yard, but we normally did not. If the mower could topple whatever was in its path without stalling or causing bodily harm to him or someone else nearby, he would usually just power the Snapper through. This strategy included newspapers, cups, beer cans, golf and tennis balls, and all types of branches and sticks.

The backyard was about an eight-beer job, or approximately three hours. He made it look like a holy sacrament to shave tiny green blades with such systematic precision, and there were plenty of days I tried to imagine the smooth rubber grip of the wheel under my own fingers, the heavy torque of the mechanical beast swinging around cleanly under my own sure gauge. Dad, up there on his mower, looked like King of Bluehaven Drive.

During TV commercial breaks, I would stare at my dad through the French doors that opened out onto the backyard as he rode in a straight line, peering between the handlebars with a beer in his hand. He powered the red-and-white machine through our yard like Patton through France, sporadically removing his LSU base-ball cap to wipe his brow, always careful not to spill his beer. Round and round he would go while my brother Tutu and I sat in love and hate, in front of the television, constantly increasing the volume on the console, hoping this Saturday would last longer than the last week's had.

My brothers and I were never assigned regular chores. We did what Dad told us to do when he told us to do it. There was no chalk or clipboard or dry-erase anything hanging on any wall in our house. It was ad hoc. Mom only had two loose rules: put your dishes in the sink and bring your dirty towels downstairs. We never had to make our beds. We rarely ate together at the table except at restaurants or on holidays. That was it.

So most Saturdays Tutu and I would sit in front of the television watching Warren J. "Puggie" Moity criticize the latest populist politician, whom he claimed was stealing from the good people of Iberia Parish. Then we'd watch some televised baseball, bass fishing, or maybe an old Western, while Bryan read. Mom would walk by us now and again, always in the midst of the same never-ending Saturday project, but for the most part, our lazing would be interrupted in these last hours only by the thump of the occasional beer can against the French doors as my father mowed closer.

This thump would be followed immediately by my mother yelling, "Get your daddy a beer." The beer-can smash was like the starting horn in a track meet. Tutu and I would quickly get up and run to the refrigerator, hoping that we could please our primary role model by delivering the aluminum can that football legend John Madden had pitched. Tutu was faster, but I was bigger, so nine times out of ten, I would get there first, even if that meant horse-collaring him and slamming him to the ground.

Opening the refrigerator, I would reach my hand past my mom's Dr Peppers, past the marinating pork chops that were to be barbecued on Sunday, all the way to the back of the refrigerator, near the temperature gauge, where the coldest beers were stored. Careful not to shake up the beer as I walked it out, I would approach the edge of the uncut grass and, standing very straight, stick out the can of liquid courage and hand it to my dad like an Olympic track star passing off a baton. My positioning would be perfect so as not to take him off his path. He would look up and smile for a second as he grabbed the can out of my hand, then monomaniacally look ahead at the uncut grass between the handlebars and the path of his wheels.

Eventually I'd make my way back inside to find Bryan absorbed in an outrageously thick history book. As I passed him, I'd ask,

"How many pages in that thing?" It would take a moment for him to rip his gaze from the page, but eventually he'd thumb through to the end.

"Five hundred forty-two," he'd reply. "Why, you want to read it?"

"Definitely not, that's five hundred forty-one pages too many."

Bryan was never one to push ideas on anyone, so he just went back to reading. Saturdays were religious for him, too, just in a different way. As a child, Bryan didn't say a word until he heard me scream and yell, and then, as Mom recalls it, "He immediately had the vocabulary of a ten-year-old." He was independent—calm, studious, and observant. He read all sorts of books over the weekend, and often sketched with charcoal and colored pencils in a sketch pad. I drew, too, but mostly oil rigs, jeeps, football players, planes, helicopters, dogs, and guns, while Bryan drew still lifes—pears, apples, vases, and sometimes portraits of my mom or our cousin Leah.

I recall often hearing Bryan play guitar as our free-form day drew to a close—he'd work on three-chord rock songs by James Taylor and Creedence Clearwater Revival, preferring the quiet haven of our shared bedroom to the rowdy clamor of me and Tutu horsing around downstairs. If I poked a head into the room to bug him, I'd always get an eyeful of the most prominent picture on his wall—Robert Redford and Paul Newman in the movie *Butch Cassidy and the Sundance Kid*, busting out of a barn, guns a-blazing, ready to meet their maker. Then I'd slide down the banister to the bottom of the stairs and tackle Tutu again.

Tutu and I were always connected, in that way that second and third siblings often are. Either I was good at aggravating my little brother, or he was very easy to aggravate, because from the time I could talk, I could look at him and he would grind his teeth in anger. On this particular Saturday, Tutu and I settled into watching

Mid-South Wrestling, home to the Big Cat Ernie Ladd, Ken Patera, Grizzly Smith, Dusty Rhodes, Bob Backlund, and the token Middle Eastern oil thief, Skandor Akbar. Bob Backlund was rumored to have a doctorate degree, but mostly, he was famous for the chickenwing. Professional wrestling was as real as a rock to my little brother.

"Let me slam you into a turnbuckle and elbow you in the back; then you'll see that it's real," he screamed passionately at me as I egged him on. I pretended to be Bruiser Bob Sweetan, while he pretended to be Doctor X. Doctor X wore a red suit and a red-and-black mask. Steroids weren't very popular then, and most wrestlers were just fat guys in tights. Bruiser Bob and Doctor X were archenemies for almost a decade; consequently, so were my little brother and I.

After *Mid-South Wrestling,* Tutu and I promptly launched into our pretend pro-wrestling match on our faux-brick living room floor in front of the entertainment center that housed our thirty-two-inch Zenith color TV and our trophy case. This was long before the politically correct invention of the "participation" trophy. The biggest trophy in the case was my dad's Leading Hitter trophy from the American Legion Baseball league, which represented the apex of his athletic achievement.

The fun between Tutu and I ended with Mom yelling, and a little of Tutu's blood on my hands. That wasn't so unusual, but this time, after I thought I was the victor, he snuck away and came back at me with a butcher knife. He was quite serious, but I was fast for a big guy. In our household we all knew that winners were winners, but losers could end up dead. I ran quickly out the back of the house, scared but kind of laughing, which aggravated Tu even more.

It was, as usual, hot and humid as I rounded the corner from the front of our house to the back and raced into the kitchen, dripping with sweat. Mom was standing over the kitchen sink, washing a yellow electric skillet with a Brillo pad that foamed pink. She stopped scrubbing and spun around to make sure that my tennis shoes weren't going to leave tracks on the turquoise linoleum. Mom had a shapely figure and was by all accounts beautiful. Some people called her the Marilyn Monroe of New Iberia.

I flashed a smile at her as I opened the Frigidaire, parched from the heat and searching for something cool to quench my thirst. I was not hungry, just thirsty. I looked past the jug of water, the premixed Tang and the solo Dr Pepper, to the red, white, and blue six-pack of beer that I had seen in my father's hand so many times. It was too hot for milk. I was sick of Tang and was not buying the astronaut hype anymore. I knew that drinking Mom's last Dr Pepper was not an option, and, well, water is water. It was clear that I had only one choice left, and in a moment that would live in infamy, I boldly grabbed a Budweiser, turned to my mother, and said confidently, without making eye contact, "Mom, I'm going to have a beer."

Her summer musing quickly interrupted, she turned to me and said with a resolute frown, "Absolutely not! Put that back!" Until the moment of her rebuff, I hadn't been convinced that I really even wanted the beer. Second children spend a lot of time questioning reality, don't conform well, and tend to have an aversion to authority.

"Come on, Mom, one beer. I'm sick of Tang, and I can't drink your last Dr Pepper. I won't drink it all. Just a sip," I begged.

"No! Beer is for grown-ups!"

"Mom, I'm almost a grown-up. Come on, Mom, just one sip?"

"Blaine, you're ten."

She turned back to the sink, turned off the faucet, placed the electric skillet on the dish rack, wiped her hands on a dish towel, and turned to face me again with one hand on her hip. I looked at her there in her blue-and-white tennis dress and her Tretorn tennis shoes, and instinctively knew that the first one to talk here would lose. Her frown moved into a slight smile. I smiled coyly back. Her shoulders dropped, and her hand moved from her hip.

"How many are in there?" she asked.

I had her! I looked back in the fridge and counted. "One, two, three . . . There's five, Mom."

She turned the water back on, looked out the window, and begrudgingly answered, "Okay, but just a sip; then give me the can."

That was it. There was no begging, no bargaining. There were no promises made with good intentions that might not be kept. She was a good Southern mother and gave in to my innocent request. I pulled the pop-top quickly and thought of the Budweiser Clydesdale horses as the aluminum can reached my lips. The ice-cold, bitter liquid burned my throat, but I drank it quickly. My first beer was gone in less than a minute. I let out a sigh and attempted to crush the can with my bare hands, just as I had seen my father do so many times before. I opened the refrigerator and moved the Tang in front of the four remaining beers, then shut the door.

"I don't like beer," I announced, and then walked three steps to the sink and placed the empty, partially bent can on the counter in front of my mom.

She picked up the crushed can, poured the backwash into the sink, and said, with skeptical concern, "Really? You drank it all?"

"Yeah," I said, "I didn't want to waste it."

"Don't tell your father," she said, regretfully.

I banged through the screen door and out into the Louisiana summer haze like a drunk slamming through saloon doors in the Old West. King, our large retriever/shepherd, waited for me, his tongue lolling and his tail wagging. Sensing my compromised state, he jumped up on me, rubbing his nose in my shorts, and easily pushed me to the ground. I laughed breathlessly as he licked my face and mauled me, smearing my shirt with mud and dirt. Dad's mower droned in endless circles around the yard as I laid my head back in the freshly mowed grass and stared up at the cloudy blue-gray skies of the delta, feeling perfect and complete.

5

Urbanites do not understand the hunt-and-kill culture of the South. Man has hunted for food, for sport, for camaraderie, and for blood for centuries. It's all ego to the unenlightened, but there is something more to it, a quickening, a language of subtle signs between father and son, signals that liberate and strengthen and, sometimes, wound and scar.

But it's hard to see anything when you're smack in the middle of it. One sunrise in 1973 my dad was standing in a duck blind in a Louisiana marsh with a duck call in his mouth and his right index finger on a trigger. He eyed the ducks over the early-morning horizon and identified each type.

"Son, mallards, seven hundred yards, three o'clock. Get down." He then blew his duck call and simultaneously tried to keep me from spooking our prey as they circled toward their watery death.

In the beginning, Dad saw the birds long before I did, but I was a quick study, and by now, at eleven years old, he was calling me "the Hawk" and "Eagle Eye," the same nicknames his father had given his mother, Nettie, who never missed a thing. Occasionally while waiting, Dad would slip from his jeans pocket the worn leather flask he'd inherited from Hop, and take a drink.

"Don't look up, son," he said between calls. "Don't move . . . I'll tell you when. They're almost in range. Let them pass one more time. You take the one on the right; I'll take the one on the left."

He never once uttered the words "let them pass one more time" without them passing one more time. He was a blood prophet. I loved hearing those words. "Let them pass one more time" meant that we had them, that he had convinced the birds that it was safe to land near the plastic ducks that floated on our pond. He would crouch down a little lower and let the Benson & Hedges Menthol 100 cigarette fall to the damp floor made of the wooden two-by-fours that held our blind sturdy over the water. With his throat strained and his gaze piercing, he would watch the birds fly lower; then his head would pivot left to right as he changed the cadence of his calls. *Kak kak kak kak kak—kaaaaak kak kak kak kak.*

I watched the cigarette as it hissed on the damp boards and I waited patiently for his next instructions with my finger on the trigger. When the birds were close but not close enough, he'd place his hand on my shoulder and turn his head slowly, catching my admiring stare as he tracked the airborne movements of our prey. Then his hands, which looked just like mine, moved slowly from my shoulder down to the stock of the Model 12 Winchester that his father had given him twenty years earlier.

"Son," he whispered, "they're right over the decoys. Get 'em." The ducks were always closer than they needed to be. Dad worked hard at making sure I would get a good shot, and he always let me shoot first.

From the earliest time in our family, for reasons I would only later understand, I gravitated toward Dad, and Bryan gravitated toward Mom. When I jumped into Dad's lap as he watched Walter Cronkite in his La-Z-Boy reclining chair in the late afternoons, our union was instant. Whenever I leapt onto him, wherever he was, it was like a hot knife through butter—he wouldn't have to move, he wouldn't have to strain, he didn't have to adjust his arms or fix his hair . . . We just fit. Bryan never fit like that with Dad.

One fall afternoon in the late sixties, Dad, smelling of blood and beer, burst through the kitchen door from under the carport. I was eight at the time, and Bryan was ten. I took my eyes off the Hot Wheels I had assembled beside a makeshift starting gate on our living room floor, and Bryan paused from his drawing tablet at the dining room table.

"Follow me, boys . . . I got something I want to show you," he said, toting a green-and-white Igloo cooler spotted and streaked with mud and blood.

Mom walked to the back door and held it open for him as he kissed her hello. It always made me happy to see them kiss. He set the green ice chest down on a picnic table on the backyard patio. I was excited to see what was in it, and stood by him like a dog stands by his master. Bryan walked out onto the patio and stood by me, curious, too.

"Bryan, have Mom get me my fillet knife from the cabinet over the refrigerator . . ."

Having anticipated his request and on cue, Mom walked out and handed the knife to Bryan, who took off the leather sheath that protected it and cautiously handed it to Dad. Dad put the knife down on the table, then took a swig of his Miller High Life and proudly opened up the ice chest.

"Where is Tutu?" Dad asked.

"He's at Penny's house playing with Alexis . . . and Deborah is sleeping," Mom said as she stood there in the doorway, the sun settling in the delta sky.

I watched with excitement as Dad pulled a dead duck out of the cooler by the head and neck and hoisted it toward us.

"This, my boys, is a greenhead, quite possibly the king of all ducks. It is also known by its scientific name, the male mallard," he said, with no trace of irony. He then carefully placed it on the cypress picnic table. I noticed its tongue hanging out of its beak, its eyes wide open. I went to touch it, but Dad quickly pushed my hand away. "Not yet . . . Wait, Blaine. There'll be plenty of time to touch, but not yet." If I were a dog, my tail would've been wagging hard. Bryan stood at the edge of the bench and stared at the duck laid belly first on the table beside the knife. Dad reached into the Igloo and pulled out another bird.

"This, my boys, is a male pintail. The people on the West Coast call this duck a sprig. Isn't it beautiful?"

"What is the West Coast, Daddy?" Bryan asked, not much interested in Dad's haul.

"It's where California and the Pacific Ocean are . . . Nice place, I hear. Lots of ducks, but lots of cars, and also lots of hippies."

"What's a hippie, Daddy?" I asked.

"Never mind. Now listen, this duck could also be called the king of ducks."

"Well, who is the king, Daddy?" I asked.

"Well, I guess it's a matter of preference, but since there are fewer pintails where we hunt and more mallards, I'd say that, around here, the mallard is king . . . Now, boys, the number one rule when you start hunting is that you absolutely must eat what you kill." Dad pushed a piece of wood out of the way with his foot and continued, "I don't know many Bible verses by memory, but one of my favorites is 'Arise, kill, eat . . .'"

"Acts 10:13," Mom said from the doorway.

"So we are going to eat these ducks, Daddy?" I asked.

"Yup, but first we have to clean them. And now I'm going to

show you both how to do that . . . so one day you can show your boys."

I caught Bryan stealing a look back at Mom before returning his gaze to Dad.

"Dad, can I touch it now?" I asked.

"Yes, you can touch it."

I grabbed the duck and began to pet and talk to it. "Hello, Mr. King of Ducks . . . We are going to clean and then eat you," I whispered to it as I grabbed its beak, opened its mouth, and began to play ventriloquist, like Rich Little from *The Tonight Show*. "Oh, hello to you, Mr. Blaine . . . I guess I shouldn't have flown into your daddy's pond today," it said through my moving lips.

"That's right . . . not today, and you also shouldn't have brought all of your friends there either," I said in a serious tone.

Tickled, Dad grew a crooked smile that slowly widened across his whole face. His blue eyes, which looked just like mine, glistened over his nose. Bryan thought it funny, too, and he laughed a little as he continued to stare at the bloodied king of ducks. Mom was smiling and giggling from the doorway. Dad's laughter was contagious.

I turned the duck toward Bryan and continued, "How about you, Mr. Bryan? Are you ready to clean and eat me?"

Bryan's smile softened, and his eyes said all I needed to know.

"I have to go to the bathroom," he said, beginning to walk away.

"Pee in the yard," Dad said as he began to pluck the feathers off the pintail's breast.

Bryan stopped, reached for his zipper, and walked toward the China Ball tree that stood by the old saggy clothesline. He stood there a moment, attempting to pee, and then zipped up, headed back toward us, and stopped.

"Bryan, come here, I want to show you this," Dad said, holding the duck up for Bryan to take.

Bryan remained stock-still, then walked a few steps closer, inching toward the duck, and stopped again.

Dad watched, perplexed. "Bryan, I'm trying to teach you something, pick your feet up!"

Dad and Bryan just kept staring at each other.

"Bryan, come in the house for a minute, I need you to do something for me," Mom called. She held the door firmly and looked straight at my brother.

"No, Sherion, I'm in the middle of this."

"Puff, this will only take a minute."

Dad's face was red, and he stopped himself from saying what he'd intended. Sherion dropped her arm from the doorway, and her eyes flashed in the late-afternoon sun. Dad's breathing seemed to fill up my head for a minute.

Mom walked slowly and deliberately over to Bryan, took his arm, and led him into the house, chatting to him about something or other—I wasn't paying attention; my eyes were stuck on Dad. His chest heaved, and he kicked something under the table that flew clear across the yard.

Feathers and blood stuck to his hands, Dad reached for his beer and drank. I watched him catch Mom's gaze as she opened the door for Bryan. Her eyes faltered as she walked inside. Then, as the door rattled shut, he turned his attention back to me, the duck still lifelessly splayed between us.

He lit a cigarette, and with some kind of grace or luck, a bird fluttered past overhead. Dad turned his gaze upward, the creases in his face seeming to settle just a bit as he looked at the sky. It was a bright day, the clouds knitted in endlessly intricate formations throughout the delta.

He gripped the duck tightly, surely. "Blaine, you have to grab the feathers closest to the breast so you don't leave any fuzz on it," he said in a raspy voice. This was the tone he used when something was important. I nodded, took hold firmly. He ripped at the breast of his duck, and I ripped at mine.

Dad and I plucked and gutted every duck he'd killed that day. We washed them down and rubbed them until every feather and every bit of blood and guts had been expertly, meticulously cleaned from the meat. We cut their heads off, and then cleanly severed their wings from their bodies with his fillet knife. He patiently and confidently instructed me at every step, and all along the way, I kept asking him, "When can I go hunting with you?" He always answered, "Soon."

After I asked "When?" ten more times, he finally gave me the answer I needed.

"Blaine, I'll take you the next time I go."

After all the ducks were cleaned, we placed them in empty milk cartons Mom had saved for him. We filled the cartons with water from the hose, closed and then labeled them with kill date, kill location, and finally the type of bird. We stored them in the horizontal freezer, swept up the feathers, washed away the guts, and cleaned the ice chest. After we finished, we washed our hands with Lava soap and shared a towel from Mom's washing closet. Bryan never returned.

That night, as I lay on the top bunk above Tutu in the bedroom we boys shared, I couldn't sleep. I knew Bryan couldn't either. His restless shuffling of sheets in the bed across from mine reminded me of the sound of the swinging door catching air as he and Mom had stepped into the house earlier that day. At last he stopped.

We listened to Tutu's rhythmic breathing.

For a while we heard Mom and Dad's voices rise in anger, and I caught a few words and phrases, "growing up," "hunting," and then finally just one word from Dad—"Bryan."

I heard the covers rustle and watched Bryan get up and walk across our small, dark room to the bathroom, where he closed the door and turned on the light. I stared at that closed door in that hallway a long time, wondering what he was doing in there, before I fell asleep. When I awoke in the morning, he was gone.

Later, I remembered Paw explaining to me one afternoon as I sat on his lap, reading a hunting book, how a wounded buck would sometimes detach from his kin and take to the wild on his own. Bryan wouldn't leave New Iberia for many years later. But some part of him left that morning and did not return.

Manhood in Louisiana is a homegrown thing. The strains of wind and heat there pull at its boys, just as they pull at the land. Revealing, over time, what's underneath. For our part, Bryan and I couldn't have been more different.

For me, like all the men I admired growing up, hunting became a religion. We'd always go on a Friday, and depending on how far the drive was, Dad would often pick me up an hour before school ended, or right after lunch. The principal would walk into my classroom and say, "Mr. Lourd, get your books . . ." Most of the teachers understood, and would just go on lecturing as I packed my belongings and walked to the parking lot.

Dad would be waiting for me with our guns and bags packed. He and the principal would pass a courtesy salutation and maybe a little small talk, and then we'd be off—driving down the old black-top highways through the marshlands of Louisiana. I'd often ask him about the drilling rigs we saw, and he'd tell me the names of the oil companies and the operators. We'd watch the snipe, the mourning doves, and the ducks dart in and out of the wetlands as we drove, until eventually we'd meet other men and their sons at a dock, about an hour before sunset. We'd load up, and then motor across a bay or wind in and out of bayous, until we arrived at the duck camp. Some of them were nicer than others, but as long as there was good food, a card table, and a bunk bed to sleep in, no one ever complained about the accommodations. Dad would always get to bed early, and he'd warn me to do the same, but I'd never listen, and oftentimes I'd stay up with the other boys, playing cards or watching TV. Sometimes I was so excited, I'd sleep with all my hunting gear on.

I remember when I was eight years old, out in the Lacassine refuge, the cold five a.m. walk behind Dad over a three-foot-wide gangplank to the docks. The north wind was still blowing blessedly swiftly through the marsh. The launch area was a beehive, bustling with hunting guides, dogs, and men. Tall boots strode past on either side of me, gear and cases clanging everywhere in discordant read-iness, and I tried to keep in lockstep with Dad, saying the proper hellos and holding tight to my satchel as the plank got narrower and narrower.

Suddenly there was a big black Labrador retriever barreling to-ward me, and I felt the sharp slap of the cold water sucking all the oxygen out of me, my rib cage tightening at the chill as my boots filled with water. They could pull me down like a stone in minutes. As I began to succumb to that dark tug, a hand grabbed my shirt collar tightly and yanked upward. Dad was smiling with concern as he lifted me from the swamp, water pouring out of my boots onto the deck, my hair plastered to my pale face.

As I glanced around, everyone turned away, and though I fought against it, suddenly my eyes stung with salty, hot tears. Because of the delicate timing of the hunt, there was a good chance I'd ruined it for Dad and me; an hour after sunup, no further guns would be drawn. I tried to stop the water streaming down my cheeks, but Dad just kept smiling. It wasn't a "you stupid ass" smile, as I'd worried it would be, but one that said "It's okay, son, don't cry . . . We got this."

All at once I caught my breath. It was too early in the arc of my childhood for Dad to fall down on the job, so we improvised. Dad proved to be remarkably resilient, re-dressing me in makeshift, oversized clothing, and making sure I got in some easy shots. I often missed. He never did. Idolatry is only good for a while, though, and unrealistic expectations will always catch up with you. Men know that.

It was some years later when, driving home from a hunt in which I took down seven mallards in an hour somewhere out in an ordinary marsh of the Bayou Teche, Dad and I took a victory lap. He just kept driving, past our turn to go home, out into the open roads of lush, unfolding wilderness. After a while, there was nothing but open sky. He'd decided something, I could tell. Cruising that flat, wide-open terrain, just the two of us, he turned to me and took me in for a moment, then said, "Son, one or two years of college is all you need, then you can work for me. We are going to conquer the world."

These were the words I'd been waiting to hear all my life. The sky looked even wider to me at that moment. I was going to become an oilman, just like my dad. This was the plan—our plan. This was what I had been born to do. It would make my father proud. And it would make me rich. I was fourteen.

6

It's hard not to get wet in Louisiana. Even when it isn't ninety degrees and the humidity is *not* at 100 percent, there's water everywhere. The northern part of the state has dozens of oxbow lakes that were created over thousands of years by the Mississippi River, some of which are twenty miles long and two miles wide. The Atchafalaya Basin, which is the largest swamp in the United States, fills the southeastern part of the state, and is a combination of wetland and river delta. Then there are hundreds of bayous and thousands of large freshwater ditches— or "coulees," as the locals call them—in every parish.

But of course, a pool, be it at the local country club or at one of Mom and Dad's friends' houses, was the most accessible and consistent treat. As a kid I had a large lung capacity, and the minute I saw any pool, no matter how big, I'd size it up and figure out if I could swim across it lengthwise holding my breath. One of the bigger pools I'd ever conquered was the one at the Sugar Oaks Country Club, which was about seventy-five yards long. I could swim some of the smaller pools four or five times back and forth without coming up for air. My mom never really learned to swim, and when I'd emerge gasping for breath, she'd sometimes lecture me about holding my breath too long . . . and then she would smile. My brothers, mostly out of envy, would sometimes call me names like "husky aqua man" or "whale boy" as I performed my water feats.

But there was one year I spent the entire summer dry as a bone.

It was the same year that Dad started making money and Cecil became my best friend.

I first met Cecil when I was nine. His father, Mr. Cecil Broussard, owned a Lincoln Mercury dealership, and his optimism matched Puffer's, so they became fast friends. Plus, there was no better time to be in the car business in Louisiana—gas was cheap, and so was everything else. Just as my dad's business rode the commodities wave upward, so did Cecil Broussard's.

The day I was introduced to "Lil-C," at his parents' house, we ate barbecued chicken, and I crashed his Z50 minibike. Everyone laughed at the bent handlebars—except Lil-C—and from that moment on, our families were inseparable. "Big-C" would throw midweek crawfish boils and steak barbecues at their home on Loreauville Road. The kids would swing in a big tree, play tackle football, and swim in the pool, while the parents would get drunk and flirt. Mom would drink one Dr Pepper and vodka, and Dad would drink as many cocktails as Big-C could mix. Dad got so sick one night drinking old-fashioneds and eating oysters Rockefeller that he vomited in their bathtub.

Even though "C-Junya" was two years older than me, much closer in age to Bryan, it was he and I who became thick as thieves. We water-skied together, I did his math homework, and we dated some of the same girls all the way through school. Cecil was larger than life. He had a wine stain birthmark between his right nostril and his upper lip, and he liked fast cars, fast bikes, Rolex watches, and the oil business.

"Before I die, I'm gonna be a legend in the oil business, a legend as a Coonass, and a legend as a man," Cecil used to proclaim.

"Cecil, you're not a Coonass," I'd tell him.

"Blaine, I don't care what my mom says. I'm a Coonass at heart, and that's all that matters."

That's what I loved about Cecil: he stuck to his guns. For Cecil to go against his mom, who considered their family too upper-middle-class to be Coonass, was a big deal; it meant, for him, that attitude superseded everything. It meant he loved from the gut.

"Coonass" is a derivative of the term "Cajun," and according to historians, the word "Cajun" is a corruption of the word "Acadian." The original Acadians were farmers who settled in the French colony of Acadia in Nova Scotia, but were then deported in 1755 for refusing to swear allegiance to the British Crown. Thousands of them migrated south through North America, down the Mississippi, to a strip of land along the Gulf Coast that stretches roughly from the border of Texas to a region in Louisiana called Barataria, at the Mississippi River, where Jean Lafitte, the gentleman pirate of New Orleans, ran a smuggling operation in the 1800s. Lafitte, like many Louisianans after him, was always revising history in the present, making up pretty names for ugly things.

Dad used to say that there were two kinds of Louisianans—those who lived north of St. Francisville, the "Yankee Baptists," and then there were our people, living south of that city, the Cajuns and the Coonasses. If you were a Coonass, then you had license to refer to your friends as Coonasses, too—but if you weren't, you had no business using the term.

Each day after school, unless we had a sports practice of some kind, Cecil and I would ride our bikes all around town. And in the summertime, before we were old enough to have much to do, we'd cruise from sunup to sundown. One of the places we'd always end up was the bait-and-tackle shop on North Lewis Street, which was owned by a man named Billy Hewell. Billy was in his early thirties, and back in the day when my dad had been a star baseball player, he'd been a four-year letterman in track and football at New Iberia High. He had wavy jet-black hair piled high on his head, which was always full of tonic, and some mid-seventies Elvis sideburns. He always sported a dark tan, and in the mornings and afternoons he drove a school bus for extra cash.

Cecil was always interested in the newest artificial baits for the waters we'd fish. And luckily, Billy had rows and rows of hooks, lines, sinkers, and lures. He had top-water baits and bottom-feeder baits for every possible fish that lurked in the delta; he had ice chests, cast nets, rain gear, and Abu Garcia open-faced fishing reels for experts, along with some Zebcos for beginners. It might as well have been a candy store to Cecil and me. However, in those early days neither Cecil nor I had much money, and oftentimes we'd just walk into Billy's store, look around, and dream of buying things. We'd talk about which lures looked the best, what kind of fish we'd catch, and how many people they'd feed.

Then, one day out of boredom, I guess, as we kicked up gravel in the parking lot, Cecil turned to me and said, "Blaine, I hear Johnny stocked his entire tackle box with stuff he never even paid for . . ."

"Really? No kidding."

"Yeah, Billy probably doesn't care. He makes his real money gambling in Coteau and driving the school bus," Cecil said.

"You think?" I asked.

Cecil kicked a particularly large rock clear across the lot.

"I dare you," he said.

"You do it," I countered.

"Man, I don't know if it's worth it . . . I never catch anything anyway. You're the lucky one."

"You really don't think he cares?"

"He must not . . . 'cause people do it all the time," Cecil replied.

"Yeah, it's only a purple worm. It's five cents."

"I know . . ." Cecil pondered it.

I thought about it a minute, then nodded at him and took off to nab something. Cecil tried to distract Billy by asking a question at the cash register as I walked back through the store and stowed in my pocket the purple worm and a reflective metal sticker that ironically read "DO NOT ENTER." As I walked with affected calm out of the front door, however, my heart racing in my throat, Billy grabbed me. Busted—and on a lark that would never in a million years be tolerated by my father. Cecil stood by me, but in the end there was no buffer for the wrath of a quasi-religious man for whom "don't lie," "use your manners," and "don't steal" were his only gospel.

Ultimately, Puffer decided he couldn't even whoop me—that wouldn't be nearly harsh enough. Instead, for the entire summer I wasn't allowed to swim. For the endless weeks that we played at pools, visited lakes, boated in the bayou, or water-skied on glassy bays, I remained dry. The only time I got wet was during my utilitarian, morning shower over the course of that entire blistering summer. Plenty of people tried to talk my father out of the punishment, including Cecil, who respectfully claimed the transgression had really been his idea, but nothing diminished my father's determination.

The year was 1975, and the country was slogging through Watergate and the end of the Nixon era, yet optimistically looking ahead to a red, white, and blue bicentennial. Dad was thirty-six and a patriot, but the color he liked most was green. The green rectangular paper embossed with portraits of dead presidents.

He wasn't alone. Throw a rock at a Coonass in south Louisiana, and you'd likely hit one who'd made it. While most Southern oilmen at the time were living fat and owned a Mercury Marquis, a Cadillac, or a Lincoln Continental, some of the worldlier oilmen in the region imported BMWs and Mercedes-Benzes for themselves and their wives. However, no matter how classy they were, or pretended to be, they still plastered their backsides with industry-related bumper stickers like "Let the Bastards freeze in the dark."

"Dad, what does that bumper sticker mean?" I asked as we headed out for a hunt.

"What, son?"

"'Let the Bastards freeze in the dark.'"

"It's a reference to drilling oil, and the need for it."

"Who are the bastards, Dad?"

"They are the Yankees . . . and the other people who are against drilling."

"And do you want them to freeze in the dark?"

"Not really, Blaine, it's just a metaphor . . . and an irony, that they need our oil for heating their homes, but they don't want us drilling for it."

Our family had new toys, new clothes, and our Tuesday night all-you-can-eat Pizza Hut meals had been traded up for family nights at Pat's in Henderson, the Petroleum Club, and other local white-linen restaurants, where we ate frog legs, fried shrimp, étouffée, gumbo, oysters of all sorts, and all the Louisiana delicacies later made famous by Paul Prudhomme or Emeril Lagasse. Like a young movie star after his first big payday, Dad—and consequently the rest of us—quickly acquired some consumer habits. Dad became a collector of Winchester Model 12 shotguns and exotic field knives. He also took to wearing *dress* all-in-ones—his favorite was powder blue and white houndstooth, belted at the waist with a small silver buckle. And he owned at least ten pairs of animal-skin cowboy boots.

He also spent plenty of money on leather goods, and belts of all types. He had two custom leather belts that he wore most days— one had "COONASS" branded on the back of it; the other read "PUFFER." He hunted doves in these belts, attended sales meetings in these belts, and went to the funeral home in these belts.

Dad found new and inventive ways to spend money—on things like shotguns, duck leases, and deer ranches. And of course, he eventually upgraded his vehicle to the ultimate Coonass status symbol: a Lincoln Continental, which he bought on a Saturday at the AutoMart. I went with him to pick it up; it was a reddish-pink two-door model with a maroon-burgundy top. I remember hopping in the backseat and looking out of the opera window. When I stepped out, I saw Dad buying Mom a new Suburban—green and white, with all the options. I watched him as he confidently wrote the check for $50,000. And until about 1985, Dad only drove Continentals and Mom only drove Suburbans.

Mom certainly enjoyed her status, too, as a successful oilman's wife. She started hanging out with new friends, congregating with the other well-to-do wives of small-town entrepreneurs, and even with the doctors' and lawyers' wives. She liked to flaunt her status at times, and though she would never say it, I sensed what she felt when in the company of certain women: *I'm better than you, and so are my kids—they're better than yours, stronger, faster, smarter.* At one point Puff bought her a gold, diamond-encrusted Rolex, and even in the wintertime, she'd roll up her sleeve to let it shine. In those days, she always had cash, always treated others to lunch, and always left big tips. She got her hair done once a week and joined a women's tennis league at the country club.

Soon, we belonged to every country club in and around New Iberia, and Dad became a member of the American Sportsman hunting club, where once or twice a year he'd go out on exotic game hunts with other aficionados. Dad thought there was a demand for a tennis-only club, so he partnered with a local real estate developer and three doctors, and they built a tennis-only facility on old Loreauville Road and called it Willow Wood. At the grand opening, Dad and the developer cut the ribbon, and they hosted a large party for all of the country club types of New Iberia and surrounding towns. Dad had a reserved spot in the parking lot and a permanent table in the bar. When we weren't involved in after-school activities, we always went to Willow Wood. We took private tennis lessons from a pro named Pete Clear, whom Dad had poached from the Lafayette Racquet Club. He was a good teacher.

I still recall the first time I beat Dad in tennis; he was thirty-seven at the time, and I was thirteen. His body had changed a lot since his glory days as an all-state baseball player; in his success as an oilman, he had long since forgotten that, at one time, he had wanted to become a dentist. He was already drunk when he took me on, confidently decked out in his tight Sergio Tacchini shorts, his favorite ostrich-skin cowboy boots, and a pair of aviator reflector glasses.

The match was over in one set. It was not close. His usual strategy of trick, slice, and lob was no match for my youthful power and the country club finesse to which he had treated me. The score of our single-set match was six to two, a sound beating from his middle son. When I proudly explained to Mom what had happened, she grinned; after all, it was he who had taught me that winning was everything. Love is so close to hate.

But then again, whenever Dad's mood had run sour, I'd usually wake up the next day to find him in perfectly good humor. One morning Dad called to me from the bathroom, "Blaine, I got something for you."

"What is it, Dad?"

"Come find out. I know you want it." I knew, as I approached his door, what he was up to.

"Dad, what is it?" I'd play along, holding my nose.

"It's money, son, plenty of it. But if you want it, you've gotta come get it."

As I entered his bathroom, he'd hand me a crisp twenty-dollar bill from the toilet, laughing. I'd grab it and run away, and he'd call, "Hey, what do you say?"

"Thank you," I'd reply through the hand that covered my mouth.

"Don't spend it all in one place!" And then I'd hear the toilet flush.

Success for some, especially for men who have little sense of the greater political and economic forces behind timing and luck, or who have little humility to begin with, can bring an attitude. Dad had this attitude, and it grew every day the rig count in south Louisiana went up. He walked differently, he talked differently, and we all began to take on his air of superiority. Of course, it didn't hurt that almost everywhere we went, he was treated like a returning war hero. All of New Iberia knew him—from the farmers, to the doctors, to the businessmen, to the bar owners—and he was quick to greet each with a grin, a funny line, or a tip.

Sometimes Dad would meet Tutu and me at the New Iberia Country Club in the afternoon to play golf. When he pulled up in his late-model Lincoln, the golf porters would spot his car early and run out to greet him. Normally, they'd have his drink poured—gin and soda or a vodka tonic—to start. Then they'd grab his bag from the car, get down on one knee, and lace up his freshly shined white FootJoys.

"You need anything else right now, Mr. Puffer?" the black man in a white pressed shirt and black pants would ask.

"No, nothing now, Butter Bean," Dad would drawl, handing him a newly pressed General Ulysses S. Grant. He'd shut the door to his Continental and walk over to the golf cart, put his drink in the cup holder, and tee off. Dad was athletic and always played a straight high fade right down the middle. Sometimes he'd let me play with him, if he wasn't with a friend or hadn't been drinking too much, and then I'd be treated the same way by the help.

"You need anything, young Lourd?" they'd ask. I'd always answer, "No, sir," as Dad was very particular about how we respected our elders.

While Dad always had a couple thousand dollars in his pocket, he made sure Mom always had a couple hundred in hers, and that we kids, in turn, had at least twenty dollars in ours. Dad bought me an orange Jeep CJ-5 Renegade before I had a driver's license, Bryan went to tennis camp, Tutu took up riding horses, and Deb began buying nice dresses and costume jewelry. Mom played tennis most every day, and we swam at the country club and charged cheeseburgers to Dad's account.

For all three of us boys—Bryan, me, and Tutu—social life progressed very pleasantly; by the time we got driver's licenses, we all had posses of followers, and we all had girls. When we congregated with our friends around Dad, he'd always hand out money and tell jokes. There were never any second thoughts for us, because as long as oil went up, so did the fortunes of his progeny.

One Saturday night as our family drove out to eat crawfish at the Guiding Star restaurant off the I-10 highway, I sat in the backseat of his Lincoln Continental as he roared the engine past the Ears bar. This dive joint was where all the pot-smoking and beer-drinking hippies hung out, sitting on their cars with their long hair and mustaches. Dad roared the car past them and sped over the gleaming railroad tracks, sending my sister drifting up above the seat by six inches; we had to hold the roof not to bang our heads. He yelled, "Yahoo!" over the blaring radio, and we all laughed.

This night Dad was particularly manic. He was singing loudly as he pulled a wad of money from his front pocket and hung a five-dollar bill on the antenna. I watched it flutter there for a minute and then fly into the wind. My brothers screamed as Dad liberated another bill; it flapped loosely into the humid night, and he jubilantly sent yet another one after it. We were beyond worry, Dad seemed to be saying—he had it all covered. He finally stopped when we turned onto the Loreauville Road near town, but not until my brothers and I had laughed till we cried, and he'd sent twenty or so perfectly beautiful bills sailing freely into the Louisiana cane fields.

That freedom. That power. That bounty. It was something I craved, something I loved about Dad more than anything. To do whatever extravagance came to mind in complete jubilance, with impunity. Almost none of my buddies' dads had a scalable income like my father. They all had allowances and rarely more than a couple of bucks in their pockets, sometimes less. In the summertime, they all took jobs, whereas we never did. I would always hear their moms talk about budgets and how expensive things were. I'd hear my grandfather C.B., who lived through the Dust Bowl in West Texas and the Depression as a boy, say things like, "A penny saved is a penny earned . . ." but the vernacular of the frugal never touched Puffer Lourd's lips.

However much he may have changed in those years of making money, though, my father's severity in enforcing rules, honor, and manners would never alter. I would later destroy one of Bryan's Christmas presents in the middle of the night after Bryan accidentally broke mine. I would drive too fast, offend neighboring elderly motorists by careening too close to their cars, and even crash my car. All of these offenses would cost me my driving or evening privileges, earn me whoopings, or worse. But somehow, none of them stung as badly as the first time that Dad really laid down the law.

That summer when Puffer ground me from entering all bodies of water was the worst punishment a Louisiana boy could get, and he knew it. When he first doled it out, I thought I'd prefer it to his usual belt beatings, but as the summer wore on, I realized I was slowly descending into a living Hades, where perspiration taunted me and my mouth ran dry far too often. Maybe in the end it was humiliation that got me, though.

One Friday afternoon, we all got into Dad's car and headed to one of his customer's camps in Henderson, Louisiana. Pat Thornton was his name, and his camp was a blue-and-gold double-wide trailer stationed about two miles from the I-10 Basin bridge. He wasn't a hunter or a fisherman, but he'd still go there on the weekends to watch TV and entertain his friends and grandchildren. The entire property bordered a large freshwater ditch and swamp; he'd built a fence around the property to keep an honest man honest, but also to keep the alligators from getting into his pool. He had two industrial fans that blew like hurricanes to keep a breeze, albeit manufactured, flowing around his property.

Pat, like all the middle-aged men Dad called on, had a potbelly and a gray comb-over; he wore all-in-ones and, of course, drove a large automobile. That day, he barbecued some rabbit that one of his friends had harvested from the Basin, and cooked us kids some chicken and ribs. My brothers and sister hopped in and out of his pool, jumped off the diving board, and Tutu threw quarters into the deep end and then dove to the bottom to retrieve them as I watched. Pat Thornton noticed the odd man out as I sat at a metal card table with my cutoff jeans and Converse tennis shoes.

"Blaine, why don't you get into the pool?"

"Mr. Pat, I can't," I said, staring at him.

"Why, are you sick or something?"

"No . . ." I said, ashamed.

"What then? It's hot as Africa out here. Lunch won't be ready for another hour," he said kindly, having noticed that I clearly liked to eat. Dad took a sip of his beer, looked at the smoldering rabbit, then at me, and nodded toward Pat.

"Go ahead, Blaine, tell him why you can't swim."

I looked at Dad, embarrassed, not wanting to admit my moral failings.

"I'm punished, Mr. Pat."

Pat looked at Dad, then at me, and clearly did not want to hear more.

"Tell him why. Go ahead . . . Tell him."

"I took something that wasn't mine," I said, not looking up.

"He got caught stealing a fishing lure from Billy Hewell's tackle mart," Dad added, to make sure I understood his position.

Pat heard Dad's stern voice and didn't look at me. He took a sip of his highball and flipped the searing rabbit with his cooking tongs. Like a fire bell in the night, the memory of being caught and seen by Dad returned, and I tried not to look at my father, but couldn't help catching his still angry face from the corner of my eye as I watched Bryan execute a perfect backflip off the diving board into the pool. It was good to be Dad's favorite, but those lines that closed so definitively against my brothers when they did not harken to Dad's call could just as easily close over me. It was lonely there. I never stole again.

7

When I was fourteen, my dad took me down to a small Mexican town called Reynosa across the border from McAllen, Texas. Dad and I had set out to go dove hunting in McAllen with his friends Red, Tony, and Jack and my friend Buck, but, consistent with the gravitational pull in this neck of the woods, we ended up in "Boys Town" instead.

We sauntered into a colorful, paint-chipped bar just across the street from Harry's Restaurant. Harry's was the most upscale restaurant in Reynosa, a place where Southern oilmen met to eat frog legs, drink margaritas, snack on flank steaks, and bullshit one another after the day's dove hunt was over. Some of the oilmen who visited McAllen every September for shooting never even aimed at a bird. They drove from south Louisiana to McAllen with an ice chest full of Budweiser and went right across the border into Mexican Babylon.

My dad used to tell a story about one of his consultants who got to Mexico and couldn't find his shaving kit. He ranted and raved, calling his wife a no-account, good-for-nothing fat cow and swore that when he got home he was going to "slap the taste out of her mouth." When he got home, he started bitching her out for not having packed his kit and complaining about how he'd had to shave with a disposable razor for a week, and how that was all the thanks he got for making a living, and on and on his tale of woe went.

She just stood there with her hands on her hips, listening to him cry "bad wife" until she could take no more. Then she unzipped his gun case and handed him his shaving kit. He never went to Mexico again, and she got a new Suburban.

At the restaurant, the six of us ate our fill of frog legs, careful not to drink the water, and after Dad paid the check we walked over to George's American Café, a hundred yards down a street marked with potholes and through a trinket merchants' mall filled with the oily faces of cheap silver and gold pitchmen. Southern Americans in cowboy hats drank beer on the street, and I remember seeing a few skinned and gutted animals hanging in an outdoor butcher shop and wondering whether they could possibly be dogs.

My father told me that most Mexicans weren't concerned with business. He explained that the bar across the street from Harry's had changed owners every year he'd been coming to Reynosa, since 1970. It was the bicentennial in America that year, so the bar had been renamed George's American Café, after the American president who'd kicked some serious ass.

Red's shirt was soaked in sweat from the hundred-degree heat as he walked next to Dad, drinking beer and telling jokes. A big man, Red stood about five foot ten, weighed close to three hundred pounds, and had orange hair and red skin. For thirty years Red had been an oil field salesman, which, in the oil business, meant "entertainer."

Dad laughed as we walked, all the while keeping his hand on the roll of hundreds in his front pocket. I laughed, too, happy to be one of the boys. Despite all I'd heard about the place, the bar's front entrance looked typical enough, certainly not dangerous in the way my best friend's parents seemed to think.

"Hey, Puff, where's your other son Bryan?"

I looked at Dad to see what he would say.

"Red, Bryan ain't like us," Dad said, in a way that made me wish that I wasn't like them either.

"Blaine, where's your buddy Cecil who drives his damn truck by my house at a hundred miles an hour twice a day?"

"His parents wouldn't let him come," Dad said. He patted me on the back a moment later. "Just us Lourds."

Red had three kids of his own, Christie, Mary Kay, and Scotty, and Red lived with their mom, Katie, whom he had divorced ten years earlier. Sometimes finances could keep people together long past their due date, but these two were amicable, so it all worked out. Red and Katie owned a large RV, and on weekends they would travel to the Cajun campgrounds and sit in lawn chairs, and Red would cook. They rarely went more than a hundred miles from their Main Street home; they didn't need to, since every oil field company worth its salt had an elaborate fishing-and-hunting camp. Red was immodest. He liked walking around the hunting camps in his underwear. Red's favorite ensemble was a pink T-shirt and a pair of Superman briefs. He was an imposing figure in this costume, and no one overlooked the fact that he had balls that hung to his knees.

George's American Café was laid out with a simplicity that belied its intentions. About three thousand square feet, the open-air bar had a rammed-earth floor and smelled of stale beer and urine. The floor was kept damp. Fred, the bartender, his barback Pepe, or one of his other boys would hose it down with water every few hours so that the dust wouldn't kick up into patrons' eyes. The place was outfitted with red vinyl covered stools, wooden tables, fluorescent beer lights, and a tin mirror behind the bar.

Red shook hands with Fred like they were old friends; he winked at Pepe and ordered us all a round. In 1976, tips from oilmen were big, so Fred was happy.

In a glass display case on the bar was some type of appetizer that reminded me of the makeshift butcher shop I'd just seen on the street. Not raw literally, but in every other way. In the center of the room was a small wooden stage strung with green-and-white Christmas lights, and along the back wall there were five doors spaced about four feet apart. The doors on the rooms were freshly painted in a crimson-red color and were numbered one through five. On the dirt floor in front of each room was a welcome mat that read, in faded letters, "*Bienvenidos.*" It was the kind of thing I pictured a Mexican grandma picking out for her front entrance. Between each door stood a potted plant that looked a lot like marijuana, and on a wooden bench next to one of the doors sat a young girl. She was staring at me.

I smiled, and she batted her eyes and licked her lips provocatively. My mouth began to water like a hungry dog's at the scent of food.

I looked away quickly, fidgeting with my hair, which was dirty blond and curly at the time because, two weeks earlier, my mom had convinced me to have it permed.

I pulled out the white plastic chair, checked it for bird shit and vomit, and sat down, cowboy style, with Dad and the other oilmen at the largest table in the bar. Dad presided at the head of the table, with Red on his right and Tony on his left. Tony was a petroleum engineer for McCormack Oil & Gas, and Dad's biggest customer. Dad and Tony met while drinking at the La Fonda Mexican restaurant in Lafayette, Louisiana, one Friday afternoon in 1974, and the two of them became fast friends. Tony had lost most of his face in a seaplane accident in 1968 when he walked down the pontoon into a moving propeller while visiting an oil well site. I liked Tony. Dad used to say that Tony was "one tough motherfucker" because he never lost consciousness as he watched his nose and half of his face sink to the bottom of the Atchafalaya Basin.

My friend Buck, who was a year older than me, sat down next to his father, Jack. Jack owned a machine shop in New Iberia where he built and repaired machine tools for the oil services industry. I liked Jack; he told jokes. His favorite joke was "You know why divorce costs so much? Because it's worth it."

Jack was a farm boy who'd gone into the navy to get out of East Texas. He spoke with a high tenor drawl and limped when he walked because a stray bullet fired by his son, Buck, had ricocheted off a rock and lodged in his hip. Jack had almost died in Buck's arms while waiting to be air-rescued out of the South Texas brush, and Buck was forever changed by the unfortunate incident. A year or so after the accident, Jack divorced Buck's mom, Lynette, who deeply resented him for it, and she later married a man who could have been Jack's twin. When Buck went off to college at LSU, I would sometimes drink highballs and smoke Virginia Slims menthols with Lynette while we waited for him to come home for the weekend.

Buck had thick, curly black hair that was square cut around his head and made him look like he was wearing a motorcycle helmet. He was short, stocky, and known to be a good fighter. Buck sometimes hung out with a guy named Keith whose older brother, Richard, was the Golden Gloves champion of New Iberia and was considered to be the Great White Hope of Cajun country until he failed to make the Olympic trials in 1976.

Buck and I drove to New Iberia from Baton Rouge years later to visit Jack at his home on the old Jeanerette Road. Jack was lying in bed in a dimly lit room, hooked up to a respirator. The curtains were drawn, and I remember Buck walking around the house, quietly cleaning things up. At one point Buck said to me, "Hey, man, go see him. Tell him hello." I was not yet versed in human death and went in hesitantly. I looked down at Jack, and he acknowledged me weakly, both of us knowing his fate. I finally spoke.

"Hey, Big Jack."

He was too weak to form a smile. He just looked at me like he missed me already as I stood there in silence and listened to his respirator breathe. Jack Phillips died three Fridays later with Buck and his sister by his side. This was 1984; the cause was lung cancer. Jack had never smoked a day in his life.

At our table Red ordered another round of beers that Dad paid for, and we toasted one another and Fred. I was happy to be with my dad and his friends. The jukebox played a Mexican jig as Red continued to order more drinks on Dad's tab. The men whispered and snickered among themselves as they eyed the Mexican hookers, who were there to work the oil field crowd during dove season. Buck and I gulped our Carta Blancas, watched the girls, and listened to Marty Robbins sing "El Paso" on the jukebox.

As I surveyed the bar, my eyes met the eyes of the girl who had licked her lips earlier. She was sitting on the lap of a very drunk man, who was wearing a brassiere on his head. She noticed me looking at her and seemed forlorn as he fondled her breasts through the green halter top that was tied around her neck.

I was not yet groomed in the particulars of high style and status, but I thought her black pants and white high heels looked fine as she walked toward our table a few minutes later with a fruity-colored liquid in her champagne glass.

Red looked at me, chuckled through his nose, smiled at Tony, looked over at my dad, then stared at her and said, "Come here, sugar."

Dad grinned as he pulled a big sip of his beer. Except for one encounter with a neighbor under a pine tree that had ended prematurely, the only sex I'd ever had was with myself. Buck and I had been joking about sex and hookers and Mexico since earlier that year when our fathers first invited us on their annual hunting pilgrimage. I had fantasized about sex with brown-skinned girls since I first studied the Japanese caricatures of men and women making love in my mom and dad's copy of *The Joy of Sex* that Bryan had removed from their bedside table.

She ignored Red and walked right over to me and sat down on my lap as I coolly laughed with Buck and my dad's friends. Buck hit me on the arm and grinned like he'd been there before. I sipped my beer.

When her glass was empty, I asked her if she wanted another drink. She smiled at me without saying a word, and Tony barked out the drink order to the bartender in Spanish. She held up the fruity remnants of her glass to Fred at the bar. A few minutes later, a cocktail waitress delivered another round of Carta Blancas and the concoction that was costing Dad five bucks per three-ounce glass. Dad did his robotic front-pocket reach and covered the drinks with a fifty-dollar bill.

My eyes caught Dad's, and we looked away from each other quickly. From the corner of my eye, I watched him take a long sip of brew and smile.

Soon, Buck had a girl on his lap, too. His date was older than mine and not as cute. Red began to speak flirtatiously with my girl in broken Spanish. I took another nervous swig of my beer and rested my hand on her thigh, just as I had done six months earlier at the Essanee drive-in movie theater with my date, Lisa LeBauve. She did not move my hand away as Lisa had.

Buck was much more aggressive and comfortable in this situation than I was. He was Methodist. The preacher at the Church of Christ, where I spent most Sundays with my grandfather C.B., said that all Catholics and Methodists were going to hell.

We drank a little more and listened to George Jones's "If Drinkin' Don't Kill Me, Her Memory Will" on the jukebox. Buck tapped me on the shoulder and said, "I'm going," and walked by us with the light-skinned Mexican girl in tow. I studied Jack's face. There was no concern, no fear, and no reservation about this moment anywhere in his eyes. He looked a lot like Uncle Bob from *Urban Cowboy* as he reached into the pocket of his green all-in-ones and handed Buck a twenty-dollar bill.

Red cackled, ribbed Buck with a "fucky, sucky, Bucky" comment in a bad Cajun-Japanese accent, and the men at the table all had a guffaw at Buck's expense. I was puzzled by the accent but grinned anyway as Buck left the table and headed toward the red-painted doors.

Red stared at me for a moment, then reached into his front pocket and handed me a twenty. This rare act of philanthropy on his part was followed by the statement, "I want to pay for breaking your cherry," a not-so-subtle reference to the virginity that I had been wholeheartedly denying for the past three days.

Dad didn't make eye contact with me as I grabbed the twenty from Red's hand without saying a word. Instead, he looked over at the bar and, in what I now believe to have been a moment of overt consciousness, got up and walked over to another table full of oilmen. Red, Tony, and Jack continued to egg me on as the Mexican girl rubbed my hardness through my jeans and gently kissed my neck.

Red continued to taunt me. "Come on, Blaine, what are you, scared?"

Jack treated us like men and was tremendously lenient with our adolescent behavior. But Dad's car was larger than Jack's, so that was something.

Dad didn't say much for the first eight hours or so. He wasn't big on catchy phrases or expounding on life's profundities in general, and I was careful not to say anything stupid. The party was over, and he was back to thinking about whatever he thought about, the sad resignation of a Sunday settling over his face on the long drive home.

I fell silent as I stared at the refineries that dotted the highway near Lake Charles, Louisiana, the oil-refining capital of the Pelican State.

At some moment, without forewarning, Dad turned down the radio. "Son," he said, "I've been all over the world." I stared at the Yosemite Sam mud flaps on the Peterbilt semitruck fifty yards ahead of us on the road from Debauchery Ville, and thought to myself that minor trips to Japan, Acapulco, and McAllen, Texas, if I had learned any geography at all from Mrs. Rapp, was *not* all over the world. He chose his words carefully, then continued, "And the best pussy I ever had is right in my bedroom at home."

That was it. That was all he said.

The silence that ensued seemed to stretch forever.

His blue eyes met my blue eyes for just a second; then he placed a smoke in his mouth, pushed the cigarette lighter in, tilted back the blue velour seat another two inches, hit coast on the cruise control, and sang along: "*Out in the West Texas town of El Paso, I fell in love with a Mexican girl . . .*"

8

At some point in the money years when Dad was bringing in more than we could spend, Mom left her old hair salon near the bowling alley for Orion's Salon on Trotter Street. Orion O'Brien was a gregarious and lively hairdresser at the vanguard of men entering the profession. He usually wore bell-bottoms and large, round, turquoise-framed glasses, and had shaggy, thick reddish-brown hair. Funny and lightly opinionated, Orion liked to chat up anyone, and his salon was like a lounge; painted in loud colors, it had overstuffed couches and a deep refrigerator full of wine and beer. People went there for more than just a haircut and a color; they went to socialize; there were backgammon and card games running at various times. He'd built up a huge business frequented by all of the nouveau riche mini oil barons' wives. When we were kids, Cecil and I used to pass by his place whenever we rode our Schwinn bicycles down to the Stop & Shop so I could buy M&M's and Cecil could drink red Icees till he got a brain freeze—it was so easy to slow your head down when you were ten.

Eventually, Mom began taking all of us to get our haircuts there. There's nothing like the fervor of a small town finding a new taste for fashion. And over time Mom and Bryan became friends with Orion and his wife. They would play bridge and go to the movies.

But my father balked. He continued to get his haircut from the old fifties-style barber near the city park. Not that he said anything specific, but you could read his disapproval of Orion in his eyes and the turn of his step.

I'm not sure he even completely understood his own objection, until maybe one day when someone had scrawled on the successful man's shop wall an overwhelmingly popular outlook of the time: "The only good homo, is a dead homo." As we drove past the graffiti for the first time, Dad's eyes flitting from Mom's look of fear to the sentiment on the wall, my distinct impression was that he was sympathetic to both. It only made him quieter.

Over the years, Bryan read books incessantly and became an A student. On most afternoons I would come home to find him in his room reading plays, history, or fiction. First it was *The Phantom Tollbooth*, and later books like *The Sun Also Rises* and *The Great Gatsby*. Beginning in about 1974, he took on various leadership roles at social and charity clubs in the community, and as student council president at our schools. He played football reasonably well, but each day out on the field, he only made the hits because he *could*. In the end, the South was no place for my older brother.

I, on the other hand, lived and breathed our bayou's rhythms, and held down the fort fast and hard. And woe to those who left.

Before the trip to Reynosa, my girlfriend, Gail Meeks, and I were inseparable. We were in ninth grade and had done little more than kiss as Cecil gently tapped the horn from the street, reminding me to return to the car—but I was planning on being with her forever. Since her eighth birthday, Gail had attended an all-girls summer camp deep in Mississippi, and through her effort and commitment over the years, she had been promoted to camp counselor. I begged her not to go. I tried to entice her with promises of Coonass excursions on the Bayou Teche, with fake IDs and frozen margaritas at Paul's Lounge in Jeanerette and weekend water-skiing trips to Lake Bruin. But she was an honest, diligent girl with highly educated parents and a bright future, so she went anyway.

I felt somehow betrayed the day she left for camp. She'd deemed us not that important. I had become emotionally dependent on an uptown girl I had kissed for an hour in a doorway every Friday night for six months.

But something in me changed the moment I returned from Mexico and stepped from Dad's car onto Main Street, New Iberia. The first thing I saw was that expansive water, bayous slipping between houses and reeds every which way, soft and ladylike, threatening to make an island of me. Everything smelled different, though the same rusted signs still swung in the front awnings of the shops, and the cane stalks still pushed as brightly into the wide Southern sky. I walked around, watching it all, the way a tourist might catalog the styles and colors of a town he'd just settled into for the evening. For some reason, I didn't smile back at the faces I knew. Cecil didn't understand my quiet.

Gail called me three times the Friday night she returned from camp, and twice the following day. Each time, I told my mom to tell her that I wasn't there, and that I'd call her back. Saturday afternoon, while I was washing the Boston Whaler, I heard the faint ringing of the phone and knew it was her.

"Hello. Oh, Gail, I think he's here now. Let me get him," I heard Mom say, throwing me under the bus. "Blaine, the phone is for you. It's Gail, and you are going to talk to her," she said sternly, standing in the doorway leading from the kitchen to the garage, holding her left palm over the yellow mouthpiece and aiming the phone at me like a gun. My heart sank. I knew I had to man up. I was tired of lying and my mom was tired of lying for me; I knew she was right.

I'd changed, in just a brief flash of time, but there were no words—to offer her or anyone else.

I turned off the hose, hung my head, and walked slowly toward the door. My dog followed, yelping for me to throw him the slime-filled tennis ball I had in my pocket. I threw it as far as I could and watched him scamper off as I went inside. Mom patted me on the back and handed me the phone. I found myself recalling the words my mother had uttered to me many times, "Without tenderness, a man is uninteresting," a quote from an icon she admired, Marlene Dietrich—but in this moment, I could find no interest in being either.

"Blaine, tell her the truth," Mom said. "The truth is always better."

Moms always know. Even though we hadn't talked much about anything, had never actually discussed Gail, I knew that Mom wasn't a fan. Gail's mom was a blue-blooded, Tulane-educated, high-society snob who thought we were a class below her. And even though arguably we were, Sherion still wasn't going to let me treat her daughter with disrespect. That's just not how things were done.

"Hello," I said, painfully. I felt like I was watching myself talk on the phone from a hundred yards away.

"Blaine! I've called you five times. I can't believe we've been missing each other. Hey!"

"Hey," I said, unenthused.

"What's wrong? You sound like your dog died. Did he?" She laughed cautiously, knowing how much I loved my dogs.

"Nothing is wrong." You always know something is *really wrong* when a man says "nothing is wrong" in a monotone. I thought of her breath, her big brown eyes, her full lips, but the breathless feeling that I'd had for her three months earlier was gone. In my mind, she'd made a choice between camp and me. She'd chosen the forest of Mississippi with fifty grade school girls over our kisses, our shared whisperings, our love for Jackson Browne, and our summer together. Or at least that was the rationale running through my mind as I spoke, with a film of hot Mexican dust seemingly never further than a few inches from my face.

"I can't wait to see you," she said. "We're all going to Lily's house tonight. Her parents are out of town. I was hoping you'd meet me there."

"Maybe," I said. "I'll see."

"That's it?" she asked.

"Yeah, that's it."

"Were you going to call me?"

"Yeah, I was," I said, looking down at my shoes.

"Blaine, you don't sound right. Are we still dating?"

"I don't think so," I said as my mom eavesdropped while pretending to clean the yellow Formica countertop.

"Is that it?" she asked again, her voice shaky and sad.

"Yes, that's it," I said and hung up the phone.

We saw each other occasionally after that at various high school parties. She was always open to me, but I was shut down. Sometimes, on my way to school, Tutu and I would drive by the Mt. Carmel campus in my Jeep with the stereo barely audible over the mufflers, and I'd see her standing there with her two best friends, Carla and Lily, in their brown-checkered skirts and white blouses. I'd nod to them, and they'd nod back. I dated other girls in high school, but in my mind there was still some unspoken pact between us that would ultimately lead us back to each other, though it never did.

I became president of the Key Club, sported Ray-Bans, and joined the pack of New Iberia High School men-to-be all competing to get lucky with the best-looking girls in the tri-parish area. More is more, I rationalized. And it felt good, some of the time. Except when the bottom dropped out, and the only thing I could hear was the silence of the water that snaked interminably around me, stretching over tree and land far past what the eye could see. That water that touched everything, so dark and beautiful.

9

One warm spring evening, Cecil and I served pancakes at a charity supper, and by then he was a devilish nineteen. I was just turning seventeen, was six feet tall, had finally lost most of my baby fat, and was beginning to think of myself as handsome.

The benefit was staged at the National Guard Armory Hall alongside the Bayou Teche, and as an active member of the Key Club, I helped host this annual pancake dinner. To be in the Key Club you had to be an athlete or extremely cool. Bryan was Key Club president in his senior year, as were Tutu and I. We felt like the Kennedys of New Iberia. We were a dynasty.

At the dinner, we wore white aprons with the Kiwanis logo and white hats over hairnets. My job was to dish three pancakes onto each plate. Cecil was to add two greasy sausages; then the line moved on. I knew most of the people in line as friends of my parents and greeted them as they passed by. At some point, my friend Lily showed up with Carla, the best friend of my now ex-girlfriend Gail. Lily was a tall girl who drove a little red Chevy truck and had a big crush on Cecil. She lived out on Avery Island and hosted parties where I drank cocktails with her mother and her father, Ned, the patriarch of the LaPepper empire. They were the wealthiest family in town.

"Hey," Lily said, "these look absolutely disgusting."

Cecil and Lily began to flirt as Lily moved over to him for some sausages, leaving me with Carla, who was next. She wore a pink polo shirt, khaki shorts that showed her perfectly round butt, and a gold Saint Christopher medal that hung purposefully out of the top of her shirt.

"Hey, Carla, how about some pancakes?" I asked.

"I don't think I'll have any pancakes, but I will have some of you," she said, quietly enough that only I could hear. I glanced up from the tin pans filled with yellow pancakes, and my face turned red as our eyes met. She inched a step closer to the table with her head cocked forward and stared at me like a lioness stalking a gazelle; then she lifted her eyelids and a faint smile drew across her lips. I smelled the soft odor of strawberry wine cooler, and I felt a tingle in my loins and waited for her to laugh and say, "I got you," but she didn't. She was the picture of innocence standing there with her Dorothy Hamill–style brownish-blond hair pulled back tightly in a white headband decorated with a little pink flower. She had one hand in her pocket and one hand on the table as she inched even closer to me with her eyes focused like a laser beam on my mouth.

"That's funny," I said, fumbling my spatula into the tin full of pancakes.

"I'm not laughing," she said, squinting as she licked her lips.

I smiled, realizing that I was soon going to have to resituate my 501s.

"Carla, are you coming?" Lily asked from ten feet away as the line began to back up. Carla never took her eyes off me as she lifted her arm and raised an index finger—*wait*. Lily looked over at me, then back to Carla, immediately sensing the connection we'd made.

"Cecil will have the details," she whispered. "I'll see you tomorrow night." Then she lightly touched my hand as she grabbed the spatula and put one pancake on her paper plate. She passed on the greasy sausages and said to Cecil, looking back at me, "None today. Maybe tomorrow."

My heart pounded in my throat as I watched her sashay away. Cecil inched closer to me.

"Bro, how hot is she?"

"Very hot," I responded, looking at Lily, trying to redirect his attention from Carla to Lily, who liked him.

"Not Lily. Carla," he said, obviously trying to redirect me.

"Her, too," I answered, trying my best to maintain a certain degree of nonchalance. The tattered June issue of the *Penthouse* magazine, which I had dog-eared on the pages of lesbian lovers in black leather boots, came to mind. I thought of Reynosa.

"What are you doing tomorrow night?" Cecil asked as I went back to scooping up pancakes.

"I don't know. What are you doing?" I asked, wondering if Lily had already closed the deal with him.

"Lily invited you and me to sleep over at her house on the island tomorrow night. She and Carla will be there, and her parents will be in New Orleans," he whispered, his blue eyes glistening.

"I thought Carla was dating Joe . . ." I said.

"Well, I thought so, too, but maybe they're not. Who gives a fuck? We are going," was his reply. I thought "who gives a fuck" was a strong statement from a Catholic whose mother thought he should say the rosary five times each night before bed, but maybe not.

"Are you going to be with Lily, and I'm going to be with Carla?" I asked, wanting to know whether he understood that I was the chosen one.

"Who gives a shit?" he said, slinging sausage onto an old man's plate. "You taught me the rules, bro. One, go ugly early. Two, big butt, so what? Three, beauty is only a light switch away, and four, it's all the same when you're drunk—we will be, and they will be."

I picked Cecil up at four thirty the next afternoon in my shiny late-model white 1976 Grand Prix with a red vinyl top and opera window that my dad and I had just traded for the Jeep at his dad's used-car lot earlier that week. I was supposed to share the car with my little brother, but birth order is a bitch, and I had no plans to let him drive it anytime in the foreseeable future.

Cecil hopped in the three-year-old car, and we slapped hands as I keyed up his favorite Kansas album. When we pulled up to the gate at Avery Island, George, the old black man who had been the gatekeeper since long before Dad had taken me there on my first fishing trip, walked out from behind the guardhouse and approached my car.

"Mr. Lourd?" he queried with a sly smile.

"Hi, George."

"I believe they're waiting for you, sir," he said. Cecil and I could feel our hearts pounding in adolescent anticipation.

"How's your daddy, Mr. Lourd?" George asked me in a thick Cajun accent as he leaned into the window, knowing exactly what I was up to.

"He's doing good, Mr. George," I said, never having been called "Mr. Lourd" in my life.

"How about Hop?"

"He's doing pretty good, too, George. He and Doc Dalton still go fishing most Wednesdays."

"You like to fish, Mr. Lourd?"

"Yes, sir . . . Love it."

He eyed Cecil, who was staring at the dashboard, then looked in the backseat of my car like a border patrol agent.

"You know what Mr. Thoreau said, don't you, son . . . ?"

"Mr. Thoreau?"

"Henry David Thoreau, from Boston," he said learnedly.

"No, what's that, George?"

"He said, 'Many men go fishing all of their lives without knowing that it is not fish they are after.'"

I wasn't really sure if he was referring to me, Hop, or Doc, or just philosophizing, so in the interest of getting through the gate, I just looked away.

"What time do you think you'll be coming back by this here gate, Mr. Lourd?" he asked, finally getting to the point. Cecil's huge grin made us both look guilty.

"What time do you get off tonight, George?"

"I get off at midnight, Mr. Lourd."

"It will be after that," I advised him, hoping this would end the conversation. George hesitated for a second and then smiled down at me with a big, gold-toothed grin.

"When you see your daddy tomorrow, please tell him I said hello." With that, he lifted the old gate.

"Will do. Thank you, George."

I rolled slowly over the speed bump and looked over at Cecil, relaxed in his seat, turning up the volume on Neil Young's *Harvest*. The gravel snapped gently under my white-lettered Armor All–ed tires as we wound our way up the road. We rolled past the old family houses set back along the turns, past the perch-filled ponds lined with water lilies, the cypress trees, and the old boat dock, where Dad and I had paddled out in a pirogue ten years earlier; past the mash warehouse, thick with the scent of vinegar and fermenting peppers, past dozens of red work vehicles with "LaPepper" stenciled in white on their sides. I was careful to maintain the posted fifteen-miles-per-hour speed limit over the thousand-acre island all the way up to Lily's ranch-style house at the top of the hill.

We pulled up to the house at last light. I looked once or twice in the rearview mirror and tried to push back the butterflies in my stomach as I replayed the conversation I'd had with Carla at the pancake supper the night before.

I placed the keys on top of the front wheel under the fender well and heard a screen door slam. Lily walked into view wearing blue jeans and a red polo shirt. I noticed her bare feet in the carefully manicured St. Augustine grass that covered their estate.

"Hey!" she said, holding a cocktail glass. I immediately thought, *Scotch—because that's what ladies and gentlemen drink.*

"Hey," Cecil and I responded in unison.

"Boy, does George like you or what?" she said, smiling with a hand on her hip.

"He knows my dad," I said, trying to be humble but also aware of my budding facile tongue.

"For a minute there, I didn't think he was going to let us in," Cecil said.

"He works for us—of course he was gonna let you in."

"That looks good, where can I get one?" I asked as she took another sip.

"Follow me," she said, then turned on her heels and headed back to the side of the house. I watched her ass move in her Levi's and heard Cecil make an approving sound behind me. We made our way up the grass driveway, past the koi pond. Giant blue irises lined the walkway. The air was thick, as it always is in the swamps.

Lights from the setting sun and the pool house refracted through the windows. The living room was filled with the sweet, pungent scent of Captain Black pipe tobacco, wildflowers, and refined middle age. It wasn't the first time I had been there. The sunlight was fading quickly, and the bamboo outside the bay windows darkened the room as though the sun had already set.

"Scotch, Blaine?" Lily handed me a tumbler full of the brown liquid.

"Thank you," I said, then took a sip and raised my eyebrows as my head shook from the jolt of the Glenlivet Special Reserve.

"Cecil . . ." She handed him a glass of the same thing. He took one sip and walked over to a turntable that was nestled among some books.

"Those are my dad's records. Not too hip, I'm afraid," Lily said.

The corners of my mouth tightened as I took another sip of the scotch.

"Not too hip?" Cecil asked, incredulous, as he flipped through Ned's collection of Tony Bennett, Frank Sinatra, Hank Snow, Charley Pride, and Johnny Cash records, finally settling on Otis Redding's *Dictionary of Soul*. He spun the album between his thumb and forefinger, blew off the dust, and placed it gently on the turntable, then softly set down the needle in the groove between tracks six and seven. He turned the volume up and then down again as the speakers at each end of the bookcase crackled. Lily and I clinked glasses as the soul master's baritone voice filled the south Louisiana night with "Try a Little Tenderness."

"Are you here alone?" I asked.

"No, Carla is in the pool house. We've been drinking since my parents left at ten this morning, and I think she overserved herself."

Great, I thought, *she's drunk and in the pool house.*

"I'm going to walk out to the pool house and say hello. I'll be right back."

I left through the back door and crossed over the creosote posts that had been laid on the ground, to the lighted two-story pool house. I could hear Billy Joel's "Piano Man" coming from inside as I opened the door.

"Carla?" I said loudly, announcing my presence. There was no answer. I walked into the room and turned down the boom box. I checked the kitchen, which was to the back of the house. There was an open bag of Fritos on the counter next to a blender. The lid was off. Next to it were strawberries, a half-peeled banana, and a nearly spent bottle of Bacardi 151. I called her name again. Still no answer.

I was full of anticipation, having thought about little else since this clandestine rendezvous was arranged the day before. She was not downstairs, so I walked up the tightly wound circular stairway to the top of the loft. My heart was pounding as I reached the bedroom at the top of the stairs. The door was slightly ajar. I pushed it open.

There, in a blue one-piece bathing suit, lay Carla facedown on the bed, her tanned legs slightly parted, her head hanging limply over the edge of the bed, and her arms tucked under her chest. Uncertain whether she was sleeping or lying in wait, I entered the room slowly, closed the door, and walked up to the side of the bed.

"Carla?" I said, touching her on the back. She slurred something sultry, sexy, naughty, and opened her legs a little more. I shook her arm gently.

"Joe, come lie next to me," she muttered.

My heart sank for a second.

"Carla, it's me, Blaine," I said, hoping I hadn't imagined our conversation of the night before.

"Oh, Blaine, come lie next to me."

"Do you know who I am?" I asked, confused.

She paused for a second with a little smile on her face and looked away.

"Touch me. It doesn't have to mean anything," she said in a voice that challenged my naïveté.

She pulled me closer, but then pushed me back.

"I'm going to be sick," she suddenly said. I stepped away as she jumped up from the bed. She stumbled toward the bathroom and then threw up in the sink. I asked if she wanted help, and when she said no, I closed the bathroom door and walked back to the main house to get myself another scotch.

I wandered back to Mr. Ned's study. We didn't really keep books in our house, and scanning the cypress bookshelves, I found myself drawn to the silence of the room filled with leather-bound books written by authors whose works I might never have time to read. I took another sip of my drink. For some reason I felt awake, wide awake.

I studied the pictures of Lily's mom and dad on a polished table in the corner of the room. Lily's family was sophisticated. Her father, Ned, was a tall, gentle man who had an easy way about him. Whenever I came to their house, he went out of his way to broaden my horizons. Every time I entered his parlor to say hello, he would remove his reading glasses, set his novel down on the polished table next to his leather chair, and stand up to welcome me.

I stood there, absorbing the essence of the room. This man had credibility and a sense of permanence about him that was nothing like the vagaries that haunted the oilmen. Dad used to say that it was easy to be confident when you had the world's hot sauce market cornered, but I knew that Ned would have been as elegant in poverty as he was in wealth.

I picked up a photograph and studied him more closely, analyzing what made me feel connected to him. I realized in that moment that it was his honor. It was the way he treated people. I felt like he viewed me as a man of quality, a man whose opinions he valued. I felt as though, on some tacit level, the man he saw in me would begin to take form through the sheer power of his subtle influence on my sense of self whenever I was in his presence.

As I walked closer, following the shelves a moment, I ran my fingers along the spines, drinking in the thick, smooth feel of the leather and the smell of history in the room. I stopped at a particular title, *All My Friends Are Going to Be Strangers*. Mr. Ned and I had once discussed this novel, about a young man soulfully wanting to write books of his own. I separated it from the company of others and slipped it under my arm.

I stood there, scotch in one hand and book under the other, and thought about my father. How hard he would laugh if he could see me now. And how disappointed he would be if I didn't laugh back with him.

Eventually I finished the last drop of my scotch and slowly moved to the kitchen, where Lily offered to cook me a cheese omelet. She and I stayed up all night, talking as an intoxicated Cecil snoozed on the couch in the presence of the great soul masters and wordsmiths in Ned's parlor, until I woke him to drive home.

"What happened last night?" he asked as we rolled over the speed bump and crossed the bridge.

"You got drunk and passed out," I said, turning up the Eagles' "Hotel California."

"No, I meant what happened with you and Lily and Carla?"

"Carla called me Joe and then puked up Fritos and passed out. Then Lily and I just talked," I said.

"You've *got* to be kidding," he said.

"No, I'm not."

"What about Lily?"

"What about her?"

"Didn't you do anything?"

"Yeah, we stayed up talking."

"Dude, what about the rules?"

"Cecil, the rules are a joke. It's not meant to be taken literally. And what rule would any of this fall under anyway?"

"I don't know—all's fair in love and war?" Cecil grinned. Then he clocked the look on my face and grew serious a moment. I knew I could show him.

"Borrowed this from her dad's library," I said, handing over the copy of the Larry McMurtry novel. Cecil had no interest in reading that book, but he could respect that I did. They say that inside every man is a small boy trying to please his father. It wasn't like that with Cecil. Cecil knew that his father had his back, and that was good enough. He lived in the moment.

He raised a brow and put the book down.

"There a reason we're doin' eighty-five?"

"'Cause I got one rule: my car has to be in the yard before my dad leaves in the morning."

"What time's he leave for work?"

"Six."

It was 5:45 a.m. as I dropped off Cecil, who made a quick jump from the car as I slowed down outside his house. The heat of the Louisiana summer sun hit me like a linebacker hits a running back. The glass packs in my engine echoed through the morning silence as I adjusted my Ray-Bans and fast-forwarded past Jackson Browne's "Late for the Sky" and the morbidly sweet "Fountain of Sorrow" and settled into the upbeat walk down memory lane of "Walking

Slow." I had nine minutes to make an eleven-minute drive. Being late could mean being reintroduced to the back of Dad's hand.

I raced the five miles down the winding Bayou Teche that led to our family home and then raced past the Dumond house, which was only about half a block away from my parking spot right next to Dad's late-model Continental. There were a couple of densely wooded lots between the Dumond house and ours. I cut the engine, turned off the stereo, and began my clandestine glide.

I passed the first lot at about thirty miles per hour and the second lot at about twenty until, just past the last tree, I could finally see our mailbox. I pumped the brakes to cut my speed as our house came into view and then went from drunk to sober in a matter of seconds.

There he was, the man who had given me the one steadfast rule, which I was about to break. He was leaning on the back of his baby-blue Lincoln, wearing his starched Wrangler jeans, a short-sleeve blue western shirt with shiny fake ivory buttons, and a nice new pair of brown Tony Lama ropers that he'd bought on his last trip to Houston. He wasn't smiling.

I bravely lifted a hand to wave when I saw him. He didn't wave back.

I pumped the brakes again, glided in next to his car, and stopped exactly at the spot where his eyes met mine perfectly without him having to move his head; it was inevitable. I wondered how harsh the consequences would be today.

"What time is it?" he asked.

I looked at the clock on my Jensen stereo cassette player and it said 6:01 a.m. I moved my jacket on the seat so it covered the book.

"It's 6:01," I said sheepishly.

He looked at his watch. He looked back at me, and he said, "My watch says six. I think your clock is fast." Dad lit a cigarette. "Where have you been?"

"I've been at Lily's house," I said, knowing that he always knew when I lied.

"Where are her parents?" he asked.

"Paris, I believe," I said, watching him closely as he looked me in the eye and didn't blink.

"Paris? For what?"

"I don't know. The mother thinks she's some type of cultured eruditic globalist or something," I said, seeing my chance.

"Hah . . . poseurs," he mumbled as he moved his head into the passenger-side window.

"Yeah, I like her, Dad, but I'm not sure the mom likes me too much."

"Well, son, she's from uptown New Orleans, and she don't like Coonasses," he said.

So far, so good, but I was careful not to overreach; I instinctively knew that I was still skating on thin ice. I waited for him to talk.

"Are you drunk?"

"Yes," I said.

"What were you drinking?" he asked.

"Sixty-year-old single malt scotch," I slurred.

My father smiled and flicked his cigarette on to the ground. "I guess that will teach those blue-blooded bastards to go to France."

10

Around the time I was sixteen, Bryan was applying for colleges, and the deeper he got into the process, the more the air seemed to thicken between him and Dad. It was like one of the swelling levees erected to hold up the ever-changing path of the Mississippi River as it grew closer and closer to people's homes—at some point, something would give. One afternoon, watching him prepare, essays and applications covering the entire surface of the dining room table, I saw from the kitchen that Bryan's look had changed. His eyes tightening. I walked a few steps to see why—Dad had walked in the room. Nothing was said; Dad walked right past him. But there was something about Bryan's gaze in that moment that reminded me of our fishing trip of five or so years ago, to Marsh Island.

The top of the Lourd line, in my lifetime, was my father's father, Hop.

Most all of the Lourds throughout time have been personable, likeable people, though Hop may have pushed the envelope on that one a bit. His brother, William, who'd been mayor of New Iberia in the forties, was especially personable, and at the end of his life, when asked where all of his money had gone, he replied that he'd spent most of it on whiskey and women, and had squandered the rest. Some might call that interminable adolescence. Others might call it wisdom.

Hop liked to give people nicknames. He had a mean streak and, like his brother, William, must not have cared much about money since he lost most of it betting on the nags and playing cards at the gambling hall with guys like Doc, Cot, T-Beb, Killer, and Lil Shrimp. He never planned much past the last race at Evangeline Downs. He never owned stocks. In his opinion, the stock market was for rich guys and gamblers. He would rather put his money on a horse at the track, where he knew the jockey and the trainer, than bet on something that was called security but which oftentimes had none. He kept all of his money, along with his social security checks, in a passbook savings account. That's how it was for Hop. He had his wife, Nettie; his only son, Puff; and a dog named Boo. Every dog Hop and Nettie ever owned was a small black or brown Chihuahua mutt named Boo.

Throughout his life, Hop owned bars, was a partner in a lumberyard, and dabbled in real estate, in addition to his lifelong love affair with horses. In 1965, through political connections, he was made superintendent at Marsh Island for the Wildlife and Fisheries Department of the State of Louisiana. The state paid him a decent salary to build dams, arrest poachers, and patrol a large area of the saltwater bay in an overpowered Boston Whaler. Hop loved being a game warden. He was always happiest alone on the water, wearing his uniform with the Louisiana state patch on one shoulder and the Wildlife and Fisheries seal—which pictured a duck, a fish, a deer, and a pelican—on the other. I used to stare at that seal in awe. It might as well have been the presidential seal.

Every August, Dad, Bryan, Tutu, and I would meet Hop at the Cypremort Point landing in St. Mary Parish, while Deb stayed home with Mom. Hop would fill up the Louisiana state–issued boat with diesel, and Dad would fill up the Igloo ice chests with

Cokes, beer, cold cuts, and freshly baked Evangeline-made bread to take us fishing at Marsh Island.

These two weeks of male bonding were one of the highlights of my year. It was a respite of unadulterated wilderness adventures and training. Dad loved it, Hop loved it, I loved it. The jury was still out on the others. Dad made us wear life jackets as we crossed the Vermilion Bay from the landing to the state camp, where we would spend our time catching redfish, trapping alligators and nutria rats, bird-watching, and eating fried food cooked by a man named Willie.

Once, after a long day of fishing on the freshwater side of a rock dam that Hop and his men had built on one of the bayous, we came back to the camp to clean the fish. Hop and Dad, like most south Louisiana men of their era, were experts at killing, catching, cleaning, and gutting all sorts of prey. They could clean a hundred fish or more in an hour, and nary a stray bone would be found on any piece of meat that left their hands as it passed to the fryer or the freezer.

Traditionally, fish cleaning always starts with a fresh beer. Hop would open up a can of Pearl, and Puff would open up a Miller pony or a ten-ounce Budweiser. It's oppressively hot and humid in the marsh in the summertime, and we'd always be soaking with sweat and saltwater as we stood at the trough. Having been on the water since sunup, we were sunburned, tired, mosquito-bitten, and hungry. But Coonass rule number one is eat what you kill, and you got to clean it to eat it. One of us, usually me, would pull the dead fish out of the blood-purple slime in the ice chest and flop it into the sink. And though I was tired, I still cranked in high gear, whereas Bryan's movements were heavy, and Tutu played at the water's edge.

On the assembly line, Dad's position was subordinate to Hop's, so his job was to cut off the head and gut the fish. I would watch him as he turned over the fish, then ran a slit an inch or two deep along the underbelly, from its gills to its tail, ripping out the guts. On a good cut, he'd only have to use the knife twice—once for the gutting, and once for the beheading. When Dad was sure he was done, he'd slide what was left of the fish over to Hop for inspection. If he thought it needed more work, he would slide it back to Puff with prejudice. On this particular day, Hop was not passing any fish back to Dad—the Coonass assembly line was running to perfection.

Bryan, being the oldest son, had the position to the right of Hop at the end of the assembly line. His job was to take the finished fillets and gently place them in a clean ice chest filled with warm water: a cesspool to some, a showcase of masterful work to others.

I grabbed the final fish from the slimy water and handed it to Dad.

"This is the last fish, Dad," I said. Then I turned to my grandfather. "Can I try to fillet this one, Hop?"

"No, it's faster if your dad and I do it," he replied gruffly, without looking up. I wasn't sure why we were in a hurry since we were on an island in the middle of a bay. But men are often that way.

"Come on, please?" I asked again, leaning in close to Hop and gripping the plywood sink. Bryan studied that grip a moment, and the keen look in my eye; it was miraculous I was still gunning strong after such an arduous day.

"No, fatso, and watch the knives," Hop said, crustily. His tone helped me to understand his position.

I grimaced and quickly moved away from the box. Dad stopped cutting for a second, flinched almost imperceptibly, and then went back to wielding the knife on the last of the day's catch. Bryan looked at me, then at Dad, and then at Hop. He then walked around the ice chest and over to where I stood, almost as if to help me see the two of them alone together. His blue eyes flashed with rage.

"Hop, I really wish you wouldn't call him that," Bryan said, glaring at them both.

"What?" Hop said, incredulous and irritable.

"Fatso, that's what. He's not fat. He's just big," Bryan said earnestly, trying to make him understand in the only way Hop could. Bryan looked at me, and if he saw the surprise and fear in my eyes, he didn't let on.

Dad stood at the sink, silent, frozen. Bryan looked squarely at Hop, his chin up and his chest out, ready to take his poison from men who were unpredictable in a culture that did not encourage debate from children until they were old enough to have no difference of opinion.

Surprisingly, Hop did not respond. He just shook his head, disregarding Bryan and me entirely, then set the electric knife down on the sink and walked crisply back toward the boathouse. Dad finished the last fish quickly and slid it over to Bryan, then rigidly lit a cigarette. Bryan peered at Dad with his eyebrows raised, then reached over and dumped the fillet in the ice chest with such force that water sprayed all over. Dad looked at me as if to understand my position, and for a moment I felt suspended in that line of heat between them. Bryan then flipped the lid of the chest shut and strode along the wood-planked path back to the camp that was raised fifteen feet above the ground on creosote telephone poles, a precaution against the high waters that always came.

He'd just taken a bullet for me. I'd never look at Hop the same way again. Bryan paused as he got to the steps, and I thought for a second that he was going to look back at us, but instead he looked straight up at the sky. If he'd been a bird, he'd have flown away right then.

11

Bryan left New Iberia for Los Angeles around noon on August 1, 1978. The white-and-green Cougar that Dad had bought for him at Mr. C's AutoMart with spoils from the oil boom was packed to the gills with boxes and clothes.

I watched Dad hug him, shake his hand, look him in the eye, and then reach in his pocket and hand him a few more hundreds before he swaggered back toward the house with a sad look on his face.

About ten months earlier—at the beginning of Bryan's senior year in high school—Dad had taken Bryan, alone, to move us into Mom's dream house, which he'd just built on the banks of the Bayou Teche. Amid the boxes, the shuffled belongings, the various trophy mounts that would hang as testament to Dad's glory as an outdoorsman, Bryan had finally summoned the courage to drop the bomb he'd been carrying around for the last few years.

"Dad, I've been thinking . . ." Bryan hedged.

"Well, it's good to think," Dad quipped while holding a three-inch screw in his teeth that would hang the eight-point buck he'd taken from the King Ranch in South Texas; it was slotted for the living room over the fireplace.

"I think I want to leave here when I graduate from high school."

"Of course you're going to leave. You're going to be the first Lourd to graduate from college," Dad said, only vaguely aware of the slight edge in Bryan's voice.

"Yes, sir, I know that," Bryan allowed, looking out the window at our new view. "The thing is, I don't want to go to college in Louisiana."

"What are you talking about? Of course you do—there is no place better than LSU."

"Dad, I don't want to go to LSU. I want to go to USC."

Dad dropped the screw from his teeth into his hand.

"In Los Angeles?"

"Yes, sir, in Los Angeles."

"No," he said point-blank, and went back to hanging the buck. Bryan studied him a minute, his rough hands nimbly moving the spiny wires into position.

"I'll pay you back. Every cent," Bryan offered quickly. Dad stopped again.

"Bryan, this is not about the money, this is about family. Louisiana is who we are. It's where we've built our name. It's where we all live and where we will all die. You belong here," Dad said, looking him straight in the eye. Bryan didn't flinch.

"Dad, Louisiana will always be my home. Lourd will always be my last name, and you will always be my father. But I need to leave."

Dad kept staring at Bryan, and Bryan stared back, hoping Dad could see him clearly. I think Puffer secretly wanted to grab a hold and shake his oldest son to his senses. As if there was a man buried in Bryan that he could pull out, wrest free, breathe to life—a man that he, Puffer, would recognize. A Southern man who was just like him.

But instead, the stare-down continued. My brother knew that the first one to talk would lose. He learned that from Dad. So neither said a word.

A quintessential difference between Dad and Bryan was finalized therein. Puffer believed in the South romantically—that the good and bad of it are inseparable, that you have to love it as it is, without asking it to change. That abandoning it is sacrilege. That sordid, uncharted places like Los Angeles, with their unhinged attitudes spinning in every direction, are Gomorrah. That there is an almost traitorous impulse in the decision to leave.

The day Bryan left for college, I threw a tennis ball on top of our home's slanted roof as Dad walked back inside our house on the Bayou Teche. Dylan, our retriever, worked his way through the yard down the roofline to catch the ball. Tutu and Deb stood by Mom, and after I saw Dad slip from the window, they took their turns hugging Bryan. I took a break from my rooftop game of catch, and Bryan and I said good-bye. As I stepped back, I was aware of the car's hum as the air conditioner worked overtime, and turned to see the cane field behind us lining the dirt road, and the stark telephone poles reaching up to an empty Louisiana sky.

Mom stood in the freshly cut yard and smiled as she and Bryan went over his last-minute to-do list. They talked for a minute, and I watched the air get tight, and then they both started to cry. Bryan turned the car off; he shut the door, and they embraced. Mom wept visibly, and I could see her face give in to his shoulder, Bryan's body shaking with tears as well. My brother finally wiped his eyes and said something to her, and she smiled as he got into his car and drove away. My mother cried for hours when Bryan finally left the driveway, as if some part of her had left with him.

I might have felt the pain of this separation more deeply than any of them. We could not exist as a whole family anymore—in one place, of one soil. With Bryan gone, we would be forced to take sides, and in this contest there would be no winners.

What had been evolving for some time now became clear: when

Dad was home, he was on the phone, sleeping, barbecuing, or cutting the grass—and Mom was elsewhere. She would putter around the house, rearrange knickknacks, or pot plants that never seemed to live too long; she'd stain a dresser in the garage; she'd rearrange furniture on the back porch. There was always more than one dog around, usually a hunting dog that was only half trained by me, and then a few strays that she picked up somewhere.

In those days, Mom and Dad only got through to each other in some archaic form of communication that was always crackly and unclear. He continued to make the money; she continued to take care of the three of us kids, and sometimes I guess they'd meet in the middle when the moon was right, but something had been lost between them. I don't know when or how, or from whence it came, but there was a lot of silence.

For a few years after Bryan left, beginning in 1980, I attended Louisiana State University, equipped with my own late-model white-and-gold 1980 Grand Prix, an apartment at the Tiger Plaza that I shared with Cecil and another friend, a $1,000 monthly allowance, and all the confidence in the world. But in the South, the storms always blow hardest after the first rains have wrecked the early crops.

When I look back now, I understand what happened to Louisiana six months later. In January 1981, oil prices collapsed. Congress under Ronald Reagan unified tax rates, ending tax incentives for drilling programs. Simultaneously, OPEC decided they would lose no more market share and began flooding the market with cheap oil.

What was ultimately good for the rest of the country devastated the South. Almost overnight, vacancy signs and Cajun tumbleweeds began to blow through the not-yet-finished country club golf developments in and around Acadiana. Whenever I go home,

I still drive by one of the cane fields on Highway 182 that was supposed to become "Mallard Lake, an Exclusive Community." It was
a cane field then; it's a cane field now. Dust to dust.

No one can predict a market top, but when a forty-five-year-
old guy named Junior with a seventh grade education has a roll of
hundred-dollar bills in his pocket that a show horse couldn't jump
over and is driving a green Lincoln Continental with a "Registered
Coonass" bumper sticker, you are probably near a market top. In the
case of my dad and his friends, it was the market top of all time.
Oil rigs stopped drilling, wildcatters stopped buying drilling leases,
expense accounts dried up, and all excess personnel were fired.

I was barely twenty and had no idea what it meant. I still had a
$1,000-a-month allowance, and Dad was still The Man. I contin-
ued spending money like a profligate movie starlet and was usually broke by the twenty-second of the month. I was industrious,
though, and when the cash was spent, I would turn to Dad's Shell
credit card and barter gas and beer for cash.

"You guys sell Dom Pérignon here?" Cecil would ask, standing
at the fluorescently lit counter inside the Shell station. First and
foremost, Cecil was a hedonist. He'd read about some oil baron
buying 150 bottles of Dom for his sixteen-year-old's debutante ball
in New Orleans, and he'd been obsessed with it ever since, even
though he'd never tasted it or actually seen a bottle. The Middle
Eastern gas station attendant asked, "Dom who?"

Cecil looked at him. "Never mind. Can I have a pack of Marlboro menthols, and whatever he's buying . . . ?" he added, looking at
me as he placed some peanut M&M's on the counter. Cecil never
paid me for anything, and I never paid him. Our money was our
money. It was community. Since we were in college, we lived on
cases of cheap beer, cigarettes, microwavable burritos, and condoms

we'd never use. But the five friends behind us were a different story. I'd tell the attendant to keep the tab rolling, and they'd hoist their own beer, burritos, and cigarettes down on the counter. Once it was all tallied, I'd plop down Dad's Shell card. Familiar with the routine, the attendant would look at me funny and sometimes shake his head . . . and then he'd ring it all up on the card. I'd just wink and grin.

Back outside in the parking lot, we'd pile it all into my Grand Prix, and my friends would proceed to repay me with whatever cash they'd wadded up. Fives, tens, lots of ones. Usually Dad and I got the raw end of the deal.

In 1982, a bull market was beginning for stocks and bonds on Wall Street, and a bear market had begun for Dad. Mom was soon asked to cut down on clothes shopping, and Deb had to quit private gymnastics coaching. That summer, he would make the first reduction in my allowance, then again several times over the next three years. I was in denial, though, believing that the slowdown was temporary and sought no alternatives.

It was around this time that Tutu and Dad really bonded at the horse track. Dad started in the horse business as a way to "shelter" some of the booty from the boom time, but quickly that shelter became his passion, and somehow Tutu got dragged along into it. They loved everything about the thoroughbred business. They loved talking about the breeding, the sires, bloodlines, the prerace preparation, the jockeys, the trainers, the veterinarians, the drugs that made them run faster or heal quicker . . . but mainly it was the horses, those majestic one-ton beauties who ran—the mares, the fillies, the colts, and the geldings. They loved the yearlings, too, and Dad especially loved the foals—watching them come out, new to life, and stumble around and then run, in that way only a foal can.

Of course, they also loved the two-year-olds who ran in the most important races, and eventually, Kentucky Derby day surpassed Christmas as the most important day of the year for them.

I often wondered if Tu liked the horses because he knew that Dad liked nothing more, and because to be with Dad, you had to love what he loved. For many years, Dad and I had bonded over hunting, fishing, sports, and taking trips with other like-minded men. But once Dad found the track, he slowly began to give up those shared interests and turned his full attention to the horses.

After high school Tutu did a brief stint with me at LSU, but there was no racetrack in Baton Rouge, so he quickly found his way back to Lafayette and to Evangeline Downs. He'd go to the track in the mornings before classes at USL to watch the horses "breeze," and Dad would often meet him there. Puffer would stand on the edge of the fence in his starched Wrangler jeans and his cowboy boots and western shirt, and Tutu would sit atop the railings as they talked.

"You think that bay colt is worth the claiming price in the race tomorrow?" Dad would ask.

"Maybe, but I think if you buy him, you might have to step him down in class for a minute to get your money back . . ."

Dad would drink coffee, Tutu would drink Coca-Colas, and they'd study the daily racing form with all its statistics from previous races for hours on end—meaningless to some but ripe with endless possibilities for people like Dad, who really believed they could predict the future based on the past. I wondered if he ever saw himself as a lucky fool when he won, the randomness of it all. Tu always understood that the stats in the form were just that—stats in the form—and if he won, he was lucky. If he lost—well, it was beautiful watching the one-ton beasts run anyway. Tu would never lose his interest in horses, and over time would become an assistant trainer, a jockey's agent, a track manager, and eventually an owner/trainer. But that was much later.

I wasn't home so I didn't witness it firsthand, but whenever I called Tutu from LSU, I heard of the increasing number of trips my father took in those days of uncertainty. A week in Houston "calling on customers." Two weeks hunting in Texas with former clients. A fishing trip alone to an undisclosed location, which was extended three times. I tried to catch Dad on the phone intermittently at home, but on the off chance that I did, his voice was either thick or clipped with that bravado men learn early and lose late or never.

Over time, I listened to Mom's voice roll into a defeated and depressed monotone on the other end of the line whenever we chatted. I'd catch her up on my classes, on Cecil's or my girl-of-the-moment, the parties I'd organized at the frat house, and sometimes the G-rated shenanigans of my "brothers."

"Mom, there is this fraternity brother of mine whose dad is a judge."

"Wow, really?" She'd enjoy hearing that.

"Yup, and he has his dad's judge directory, and sometimes late at night when he gets back to the house from Murphy's . . . he'll crank-call some of the other judges."

"Blaine . . . you are kidding me," she'd say, laughing.

"Nope, and some of them will talk to him."

"What does he say to them?"

"He says things like this—and sometimes worse—'Yo, Judge, I saw you with your secretary at the bar. Put the money in the box.'"

"Who is this?" the judge would ask.

"Don't worry about who this is. Just put the money in the box," Robert would insist with a quick cough.

Sometimes these paranoid judges would talk to him for ten or fifteen minutes before Robert would get bored; at the end of the call, Robert would always just start laughing and tell them to watch themselves. But sometimes, the judge would say, "What box, where?" and Robert would make up a location before he hung up. I always wanted Robert to call *his* dad, but Robert never went for it.

Meanwhile, in our phone conversations, after we'd covered all current events, Mom would ask me when I was coming home. I'd always say, "Maybe next weekend, but definitely over the holiday." In those last years of college, at the end of the call when she said "I love you," it began to sound like "save us, please."

As Mom and Dad's bank balances dwindled, so did their moods and attention spans. At some point, all that was physically left on our stretch of the road was a fishing boat in the yard that never got used, a few stray cats meandering in the garage, an overgrown flower bed, and a little girl who was becoming a woman, Deb.

Deb was a charming, smart girl in the middle of high school, but amid the dark cloud that hung over Mom and Dad, and with all us boys pretty much grown up and gone, she had to find new ways to entertain herself. She got a driver's license, quit dance and cheerleading, picked up a beer and a cigarette, and began to grow up fast.

Though Tutu was mostly living upstairs in our house, after leaving LSU he'd grown increasingly detached from the day-to-day goings-on in the Lourd home. He woke up early, went to classes at USL, worked at the track as a stable boy, and when he was home kept his door closed. Tutu reported, when I talked to him, that Dad took lots of naps and was spending more time on the couch.

I decided to get him off of it. I knew Dad loved the Mauberret family.

One of the great things about going away to school and joining a fraternity, for a small-town boy, is the new friends you can make. Judges' sons, appliance salesmen's sons, divorce lawyers' sons, and bigwigs' sons. One of the guys I met and became real friendly with was a fellow from New Orleans named Claude T. Mauberret. His dad, Dr. Mauberret, married late and didn't have kids until he was fifty, a rarity in those days. He was the New Orleans fairgrounds veterinarian, a snappy dresser, and had been elected tax assessor for the French Quarter in New Orleans. Dr. Mauberret lived uptown near St. Charles, by Tulane and the streetcars, but he also owned a large section of land across the lake in a little farming town called Lacombe. The Mauberrets farmed beans and raised horses there, but mostly used the land as their private hunting grounds. In the fall, they'd flood a few ponds with water from the nearby bayou and shoot ducks, and they'd plant millet in their pastures so they'd be able to shoot doves.

Claude and Dad had a mutual admiration for ponies and whiskey, and ever since they'd met at a fraternity house parent function, they were fast friends. Claude knew that Dad loved to drive the causeway bridge and hunt doves, so if I got invited to shoot, he'd always say, "Please tell Puffer to come along." In this cycle of the oil downturn, I called Dad a few times about Claude's upcoming shoot, determined to catch him at home. When I finally did and we spoke, Dad gladly accepted the Mauberrets' invitation.

Every hunting season, or split in a hunting season, opens on a Saturday. This particular Saturday, we'd arranged to meet Dad at the 7-Eleven right off the I-10 bridge near the Bonnet Carré Spillway, about ten miles from Lacombe. Dad was always a prompt man, but something told me as we pulled into the parking lot that day that he'd probably been sitting on the hood of his 1981 blue-on-blue four-door Lincoln Continental for at least an hour.

All my friends called Dad "Puff" or "Puff-n-Stuff," and as we greeted one another that crisp autumn morning, we shared a few jokes and refilled our ice chests. Dad seemed a little preoccupied, but I didn't pay much attention to it, as back then there was nothing a good flock of doves couldn't cure. I cracked open a morning beer, pinched a big chunk of Skoal between my front teeth and gums, and told him to follow us. We rolled up to a chain-link fence, and once I opened the gate, I waved Claude on and hopped back in the car with Dad. As my father and I watched the mourning doves work the fields, we inched the car forward, excited—knowing this was where we belonged.

Dr. Mauberret and a few of his compatriots had already marked their territory in the large field and were waiting for the clock to strike noon, when the shooting could begin. As we parked, Dad popped the trunk on the Lincoln and slowly slipped on his old khaki Beretta shooting vest, the one he'd worn on every dove hunt we'd ever been on together. He took off his cowboy hat and slipped on an old-school camouflage baseball cap, then lifted up a blanket that hid his south Louisiana arsenal and handed me a gun.

"20-gauge Model 12?" he asked, as he cracked open the breach.

"Isn't this Tutu's gun, Dad?" I asked, admiring the blue steel barrel and the varnished stock.

"Yeah, it's the gun I bought him for Christmas in '77. I don't think he's ever used it," he replied, somewhat disappointed.

"Well, Pop, I sure will," I said as I grabbed two boxes of federal express dove load from the case.

"Puff, I got you a spot right by your car." Claude smiled, motioning to a cypress leaning mightily to one side, full of kudzu and stray millet tufts. "You see that tree? I set up a little chair and put six Coors Lights in that camouflage cooler. And trust me, you won't have to even stand up to shoot your limit," Claude said proudly. Dad barely nodded and walked slowly over to the dwarfed folding chair quaintly erected under the massive cypress. Claude didn't seem to notice, though—his gait crisp and eyes alight as he moved west toward another stretch of the field.

"Blaine, you're with me, let's take a walk," he intoned; I looked back as I followed him into the bush.

"Dad, you good here?" I asked, feeling a little older for some reason.

"Yes, son, I'm good. And thank you, Claude."

"Sure thing, Mr. Puff. See you in a bit!"

Claude and I walked to the end of the three-acre brown top millet field, the noonday sun hitting, guns starting to shoot, and birds starting to fly. Each shot I took, though, somehow lacked that snap—that satisfaction that usually seemed to rip through the air, to the bird, and right back to me. I wasn't off my game, though; I had my twelve birds in less than an hour, and a couple of the doctor's friends congratulated me. Claude was four or five birds short when I left him in the field and, with a growing intensity, began to walk back toward Dad.

As I kicked my hunting boots sharply through the grass, I saw my father standing about fifty yards from his chair. His gun was on his shoulder, and he was staring up toward the sun openly—it reminded me of what parents tell kids not to do, look too directly into those blazing rays. Birds were flying all around him, but never did his head move and never did he raise his gun. I stopped and watched him, waiting for him to move. He didn't. He held his cap in his hand, his hair gently blowing in the October wind, face to the heavens, his eyes now closed and soaking in the sun. A cacophony of shotgun blasts and BB chatter pattered around me in the fields.

I again moved toward the man who'd taught me to love and respect the divinity of nature on days like this.

"Beautiful day today, isn't it?" Dad said as I reached him.

"Yes, it is," I said, startled by his introspection. "Did you get your limit, Pop?"

"Nah . . . I shot a few times. I think I got six or so. You want to kill the rest?"

I stared at him. "Dad," I said, quietly, "you've never, ever offered me birds before. You okay?"

"Son, I never had a bad day," he said with what looked, for the first time, like a salesman's smile. I found myself motioning to his glasses, which had slipped on the bridge of his nose; he absently fixed them.

"Hey, why don't you take three, and I'll take three," I suggested.

"Yeah, that's good," he replied indifferently, and just like that, he put his gun to his shoulder and shot twice, killing a pair dead. Both birds fell to the ground with a thump and roll of feathers. Dad pumped open the Model 12, as a little smoke floated out of the barrel, and began the short walk to pick up the delicate prey.

And just like that, he declared into the wind, though I could not see his face, "Hey, son, you take four. I'm done."

I watched him walk slowly over flattened grain stalks to pick up the kill. He bent down, placed a knee on the ground, and gathered the first of his harvest, staring at it a moment, his eyeglasses again sliding. He stood up and pushed them into his vest pocket. Then he walked a few steps more, gathered the second dove, slid it into the kill pouch, and walked the twenty-five feet to his chair under the tree. He opened the breach of his gun, laid it on the ground, flopped down on the chair, took off his cap, and crossed his feet.

After we'd had a few beers and had begun to organize our

cars to leave, Dad asked me to meet him at the nearby zydeco bar, Last Chance, for a drink before his long drive west to New Iberia.

As I sat on that bar stool and listened to Rockin' Dopsie sing, I pondered the man before me. It was 1984 and the moment in which I finally came to the realization that the dream was over. In fact, looking back, I think Dad came to that hunt to communicate that to me somehow.

"That was fun, Dad. More birds than I expected," I said, watching him touch his dry hands to the wooden lip of the bar. "And you shot well, as usual. Wish we could do it more often," I added. His mind was elsewhere; he slowly shifted to pull himself closer to the bar.

The bartender walked over and asked, "What'll you have, sir?"

"A Miller Lite." The bartender retrieved and twisted off a longneck, then set it down in front of Dad.

"You all right?" I asked.

"Yeah, I'm all right." He seemed to be studying an old man sitting opposite us in the corner.

"The business will come back. It always does," I said, hoping he couldn't hear the doubt in my voice. He took another sip of his beer and reached for the peanuts on the bar, popping a few in his mouth. I grabbed some nuts, sat a little more upright, and took a swig of my beer.

"Dad, a couple more semesters of school, and I'm gonna graduate. The people you can't call, I will. We're gonna make it."

He didn't respond.

The jukebox played Charley Pride's hit "Kiss an Angel Good

Morning," and that old man across from us dragged his elderly wife onto the dance floor. They started a gentle Texas two-step, alone, at three o'clock in the afternoon. Dad looked at them, and his lip crinkled into a small smile. I thought of a line I'd read somewhere: "Life is terrible. Ain't it grand?"

Then he looked at me and said, "Son, it's important that you finish school. Please tell Claude thanks again for the hunt." He downed the rest of his beer, then slowly stood up, a little less upright than I remembered. He reached in his pocket for the ever-present roll of hundreds, and as he pulled it out, I noticed it was sparse. He undid the rubber band, slapped down fifty on the bar stool, and said, "Keep the change. Don't forget to call your mother." We shook hands, and I watched him slowly drag his heels out of the bar.

Ultimately, in the shakeout that ensued, 75 percent of all the small oil companies and service providers in Louisiana would go bankrupt. The savvy businessmen filed early, holding on to some of their assets in reorganization. The more prideful ones, like my father, considered bankruptcy a breach of honor, and so naively faced trying to survive a ten-year bear market. Changing something about the way he did business would be admitting to a flaw in its design, and so, like much of the South, Puff poured endless faith into the idea that he had been right in the first place and changed nothing. Until his bank account bled out.

And so, almost overnight, the *things* that made us happy in the early seventies, if only for a minute, were gone. The banks soon owned all the Lincolns, the ranches, the Beechcraft King Airs, and the duck camps. The banks were also in trouble, as they had been lending money to the oil business based on projected oil prices of sixty dollars a barrel. Projection, pro forma, and extrapolation—predicting the future based on the most recent past—is a misguided science. Sentiment had been far too bullish; nothing is more deceptive than an obvious clue.

Two-thirds of the people in Louisiana, Texas, and Oklahoma had been directly involved in oil. The smart men had saved their money, preparing for the rainy day. Problem is, it always rains a lot longer and harder than you think it will. Dad had saved a lot of money, but in the end, it wasn't enough to conquer his disappointment.

It didn't happen all at once, but slowly over a number of years. In the beginning it was just the three-year-old cars in the driveway that didn't get replaced. It was the flat tire on the boat trailer that never got fixed. It was the wooden garage door that came unhinged in one of the tropical storms that never got rehinged. Dinners out were replaced by takeout, and then home cooking, which meant Mom ate alone more often. Instead of a hundred dollars spending money, Dad was giving Sherion forty bucks, which stung, given she'd become accustomed to a consumer lifestyle.

The Willow Wood club, which Dad had founded in the glory days with friends, didn't fold because they'd already bought and paid for the land. However, all around the club, weeds grew up and covered things; they stopped putting fresh gravel in the parking lot; the paint around the clubhouse faded and chipped. Where the tennis courts got cracked and the lines got blurred, they stayed cracked and blurred. Nets on the far tennis courts that needed to be replaced never were. The bar was always stocked up, though. They couldn't shut it down for the longest time because Dad—

along with most Coonasses, deep down—harbored this overbearing feeling of being "less than," and closing the doors would prove the point.

He would always go to New Orleans to buy a car when the same, exact cars were available in town. When I was told I could never play football again, that it was like playing Russian roulette with my spine, Dad made me go all the way to New Orleans to see Dr. Jones—who immediately said, "Harvey, why'd you come here? Smartest doctor I know, Dr. Lee Sonnier, number one in our class, is from New Iberia—why didn't you just see him?"

Dad had no answer for that, because when you're compensating, you never talk about it. Around the jovial smiles of even the brightest Louisianans, every once in a while lurks an occasional provincial, parochial, paranoid insecurity. From that place comes the need to keep every last soul on the same page, whether it be where you buy your car, drink your wine, or say your prayers. It just didn't get easier as the resources dried up and rolled away. In those years, eventually Dad couldn't look Mom in the eyes the same way.

Puffer would never again walk with his head high, and his eyes would never again twinkle quite as blue. At forty-five years of age, his life began to unravel. He began answering every courtesy salutation with the rote lie "I never had a bad day." Every time I heard him say it, it depressed me. We would never again talk about being business partners.

Four years into the bear market for crude, on Thanksgiving Day, he wrote a note and left it on the kitchen counter for all of us to read.

The Lourd Family—

Being in business: No person in the Lourd family has ever successfully retired from business. We are like the hammer that breaks. I hope you will be like the anvil that doesn't.

Love, Dad

12

These were the conditions that prevailed: failure was not an option. Looking for a job became an obsession. Industries with growth potential were my focus, and I applied for countless positions at all kinds of firms from Louisiana to Texas. Feeling I couldn't risk upsetting Dad, who appeared and disappeared with great frequency and little more than a distant salutation, I did all of it solo. But nothing hit.

With so much time on my hands, I couldn't avoid the months-standing invitation to visit Hop and Nettie any longer, so one afternoon while dropping "refresher" résumés off at companies I'd already visited—and being curtly dismissed at a few desks—I finally stopped in at their dilapidated, one-story home.

Once again, they had a small, black Chihuahua-like dog named Boo. This Boo, like all their previous Boos, never ate dog food. She had her pick of anything Hop and Nettie ate, mostly ice cream sandwiches, cheeseburgers, eggs, bacon, or toast from Hop, and cold cereal or peppermints from Nettie. And this happened to be the fateful day when this particular Boo met her demise in Nettie's room.

Hop was seated on the bed next to Nettie, and I was sitting in Hop's leather chair next to the bed with Boo on the arm of my chair, eyeing me with suspicion as I taunted her with sotto voce whistles that neither Hop nor Nettie could hear. I had to do something to ward off the stagnant air permeating the house.

I looked up at the wall above Nettie's bed, where she'd hung a fluorescent light that she used to read the arrest report in the *Daily Iberian*, and recognized, below it, three palm leaves that had been tacked to the wall since a Palm Sunday service some years earlier. Back when I was in high school, if I recall correctly. To the left of her bed was a portable toilet to which I dared not get too close.

We had talked through our usual topics—hunting and fishing and LSU football. Nettie told me how good I looked and called me by her brother Robert's name for the first ten minutes of my visit, and then the conversation turned briefly to Bryan and then to Tutu and, of course, to horses.

"Blaine, I wish your brother didn't like them horses so much. Nothing good ever happens at that track. I guess he gets it honestly, though, from your dad and Hop."

"Maw-Maw, Tutu is doing good."

"That's no way to make a living, betting on the nags, staying at the track. I wish God never made horses."

Hop and I ignored her as she went on mumbling until the country dance channel again caught her eye. The conversation slowed for a moment. I gazed up at the palm leaves and then turned to the Magnavox. Hop offered me some coffee.

"Sure," I said, "if it's not too much trouble."

"No trouble at all," he said, and stood up slowly, moving his aluminum walker in front of him as he shuffled forward with great effort. For a moment, I pondered the great leveler, time. Boo jumped down from the chair and back-stepped slowly in front of him, anticipating the trip to the kitchen and food. I looked down at the dog and knew that this was not going to be the fastest cup of coffee of my life.

Suddenly, the left leg of Hop's walker snagged on the carpet and sent him tumbling forward. It happened too quickly for me to react: Hop and the walker fell like one of the great oaks of the Bayou down onto the dog. Boo froze as her life of burgers and ice cream flashed before her swelling eyes. Hop murmured a frightening "Goddamn" as he tumbled forward, and the front bar of the walker slammed squarely down into Boo's throat. Then, without one yelp, it was over; the dog was dead. Blood spewed from her small mouth and onto the carpet that had been there since Eisenhower was president.

I pulled Hop up and helped him into his chair. He was flustered and shaking. Nettie tried to sit up but, thankfully, could not see over the edge of the bed. I wished Bryan could have been there to soothe their hearts and clean up another Lourd family mess and deliver them a new, fat, half-breed Chihuahua. All I could think as I walked out of their house is that, someday, this could be me.

At last, unable to find anyone to hire me, demoralized and running out of options, I called Bryan, who, in completing his studies at USC, had been fully bitten by the showbiz bug.

During his first few months living in LA, Bryan flourished—so many different perspectives, creative energies, and people of all nationalities living in this dense yet sprawling, eclectic suburb they called a city. USC was an anomaly itself, nestled near South Central, drawing upon the multifaceted business verve of downtown and yet far from the currently acknowledged creative power center of Los Angeles: Beverly Hills. While still an undergrad, Bryan thrived networking with the student body and faculty. He organized Songfest, the largest student-run live-music event in the country, and studied film religiously. When he graduated, he first went to work as a page for CBS studios and then landed one of the most coveted entry-level jobs in the business, as an agent trainee at the William

Morris Agency. He became the first man in the Lourd family to graduate from college, and certainly the first to ever wear a suit and tie to work.

It was a rough climb. Calling one afternoon from LA, Bryan confided, "This job isn't so glamorous. I work fifteen-hour days, almost for free, and my 'official' business consists mostly of fetching coffee, copying scripts, screening calls, and picking up the dry cleaning." He sighed. "*But . . .* I got to talk to Paul Newman yesterday." And I could hear the smile in his voice. Though there was literally no limit to what some agents made their trainees do, Bryan was one of the lucky ones—his boss, Larry Auerbach, always treated him with respect, and ultimately became his mentor. Treating him like a son, Larry would sometimes take Bryan out to lunch if his calendar freed up, or invite him for Sunday dinners.

For me, the whole experience sounded surreal; during every conversation in which Bryan said the word "agent," I always thought of Maxwell Smart, and then James Bond. I'd never become too enthralled with stardom or Hollywood. Yet I called him one day after too many beers and a long afternoon of getting nowhere hunting for a job in the ever-dwindling oil patch, and he graciously invited me out for a visit. Even though Dad hated Los Angeles and would've snubbed my decision, I filled an overnight bag and flew standby on a packed 747 flight the very next day.

When the plane landed, I walked down to baggage claim and almost didn't notice the suited man holding a cardboard placard with my last name scribbled on it. I looked over at him; he looked to me.

"Hey. My last name is Lourd. Are you waiting on me?"

"Indeed, Mr. Lourd, welcome to Los Angeles. Let me help you with your bags."

So this was how the gates of hell were greased.

Bryan threw a small party in my honor at his favorite bar, Joe Allen's, which was the perfect place for a guy like me who was trying to fill the hole in his soul with whiskey, women, and boyhood dreams of wealth. The place was filled with utilitarians in search of the LA dream, which, as far as I could tell, was simply fame. Actresses in the prime of splendid desperation were milling about in their endless search for the best agent, the best manager, the best haircut, the best publicist, the best tits, the best ass, and, most important, the guy in the best position to get them on the cover of the magazine of the moment. The close-ups for which most of them were waiting would never come. Time would wear on, and they would use every means possible, probably breaking the hearts of good men along the way, to postpone the inevitable. Dad had warned me about this city.

I had a good enough time, though, and by the end of the night wound up in the bed of one of the aforementioned starlets, definitely doing nothing to further her search.

That Sunday, Bryan and I met one of his friends, Andrew, for brunch at a restaurant called Le Petit Four on Sunset Boulevard. Bryan had just gotten his first car allowance from the agency, and had subsequently picked up a four-door 190E Mercedes-Benz. It was the first black car I'd ever set foot in, though I soon realized 80 percent of all cars in Hollywood were black. In it, Bryan had a phone, which he was careful to use only when absolutely necessary, as his expense account was meager. We listened to Robert Cray's "Strong Persuader" as we drove from his one-bedroom apartment on Orlando up San Vicente, then down La Cienega, passing what was arguably then the retail capital of the world, the Beverly Center. Next, we ascended to Sunset Boulevard, passed Tower Records, the music venues and bars, the edgily dressed hipsters, and the endless specialty eateries. I realized in that moment that you cannot ever feel a city, truly, until you drive its streets. No amount of books read or words heard can get you there . . . You just have to live it.

I had a cup of black coffee sweetened with this new, blue-packeted substance, Equal, said good-bye to Andrew, and we drove west to Venice Beach, where Bryan bought me a funky Venice Beach T-shirt. We watched the dudes pumped with steroids lift weights and Rastafarians skate and play guitar. The sun shined brightly, a breeze blew, and to top it all off, I had my picture taken with life-size Ronald Reagan, Jimmy Carter, and Anwar Sadat cardboard cutouts. We sat at a Venice Beach Boardwalk bar, drank a few beers, and ultimately Bryan offered that if I wanted to move out there myself, I could share his apartment until I could afford one of my own. It was hard to fathom that he had such strong, real footing in this land of make-believe, but nevertheless he did, and I really had to think about it.

As we proceeded to drive east from the Pacific Ocean, I started to feel more at ease with the endless traffic lights, the swaying palm trees, the hundreds of faces perpetually shrouded by sunglasses, and the vast stretches of highways pooling myriad fiefdoms into one far-reaching mass of chaos and competing interests. Bryan read a script when we got home, and I took a nice, long nap. We ate pasta that night at Hugo's and I slept like a baby on his rolled-out futon.

The next morning Bryan woke me up with a cup of fresh-pressed coffee and a bran muffin, my first of each, and took me to the airport early so he could make his eight a.m. staff meeting at the ten-percentary of the moment. Driving south on the 405 toward LAX broadened my sense of the region; it was not a system of bayous or waterways; it was a system of freeways that threatened to claim everything as far as the eye could see. There was no suggestion of a beginning or end, just people and cars in flux, mostly passing without touching. I squinted a moment, feeling for the takeaway, but couldn't find one. It sure was sunny, though. Bryan hurriedly weaved the 190E in and out of traffic, rushing up to the curb at Continental Airlines. I hopped free, grabbed my camouflage duffel out of the backseat, and hit the inside of the door.

"Call me when you get home," he said, seeming a little sad behind the clip-on shades.

"I will, man. Thank you for everything."

"*Mi casa, su casa*," he added with a grin, pulling out fast as he issued one more horn beep and a final hand wave from the sunroof. I walked through the automatic doors and picked up my boarding pass. I strolled to my gate about two hours early for my flight, took a seat, and watched the parade walk by, trying to imagine myself living here. Something in my gut told me I had to try.

When I returned to Louisiana, however, the rich air filled my lungs, a tantalizing reprimand for having strayed, and I began to doubt myself.

That night as I lay in bed, listening to the air conditioner hum and the squirrels chase each other in the big oak trees that lined our backyard, I asked myself whether I could truly leave this place. I remembered Paw-Paw Brice saying, "Don't mess with happiness. Once you leave, you can't go back."

That wisdom scared me. Leaving here would be like leaving my own skin. I lay quietly in the dark, my chest tight. Like my brother before me, I wrestled back and forth with the sheets, their fabric irritating me regardless of where I lay. The bunks were gone, I had the room all to myself, and yet I got up and walked to the bathroom, turned on the light, and stared into the mirror.

There was no answer in the stark reflection that stared back at me, blinking in the brightness. I switched the light off again, slapped water onto my face, and stood there in the bare moonlight, hating what I was even considering. And yet, if I stayed, where and how would I succeed?

In the morning, the tension rose in the back of my neck at the thought of facing Dad. I took a slow, hot shower, attempting to calm my nerves, got dressed, and went downstairs.

Every moment, every question, every encounter between Dad and me was a test. It was not like math or science; there were no fixed equations or rules. Depending upon the situation, he could answer the same question in three or four ways from one day to the next. These tests had no grades. And you never really knew if you passed, but failure was quickly understood. It could be met with the crack of the belt, the lash of the tongue, or, worst of all, the silence of disappointment.

As I approached Dad in the garage that morning, I found him sharpening his lawn mowing tools, which still gleamed as pristinely as ever, shouldered by a multitude of weed whackers all competing for his attention.

Looking at him, hair in his eyes as he worked, I wanted so badly to take a seat on Mom's old abandoned saddle and just soak up the nuance of blade repair, as I had in years past. But a sharpness was there in my throat that I couldn't ignore, so I quickly cleared it and made my entreaty.

"Dad, I think I'm leaving," I said, my voice sounding strange under the weight of my words. I couldn't look at him, and studied the cracks in the worn-out cement flooring. When I looked up, he hadn't stopped working and seemed unaffected.

"Where are you going, son?"

I took a deep breath.

"Bryan thinks I should come to Los Angeles because there are more opportunities there. I'm thinking of going into banking. Maybe securities. Maybe I'll be a stockbroker, like your friend Jeb—isn't that his name?" I clarified.

Now Dad stopped, put down his Poulan, stood to his full height, and stared at me, enraged.

"Motherfucker, Blaine. *You're* leaving? And to become a two-over-prime cocksuckin' LA banker? What happened to you, man?"

He spun away quickly and cranked the weed trimmer, a cloud of blue smoke rising up and trailing him as he walked away.

Then I heard the engine rev, the fishing line hitting the weeds on the edge of the house and flatly discharging them. Thrashed at their roots, the once verdant stalks lay lifelessly below. I felt strangely empty as I stood and walked unsteadily back into the house, through it, and out the front door. It's hard to know where you're going when you suddenly don't know where you're from.

My harsh emergence into manhood was enacted in damp fields over dead carcasses and the squeal of waterfowl plucked from the sky by shotguns inherited from relatives gone, in the parlance of profanity and innuendo played out by men in hunting lodges away from their women. There was little discretion. The rules were simple. If you were old enough to be there, you were old enough to hunt, kill, curse, fuck, and feast on the prey.

This was the way of the South of my youth, boys walking in the footsteps of men who themselves did not know the way or who, in some primordial wisdom, instinctively held to the truth that trudging through the fertile, teeming marsh of life itself was path enough. And if you happened to be the son of a man like that and asked, someday, over the carcass of a whitetail deer shot point-blank for sport by men like that, "What can I do with this? What should I know? What does this teach me?" you break a code so written into shadow that no path you'll ever choose, no fortune you will ever earn, can lead you back to what it means to be a son who follows in his father's steps and so becomes a man.

13

I drove through the night to El Paso, listening to Merle Haggard, Stevie Ray Vaughan, and Jackson Browne. The radio in the hatchback had been stolen, so I had only a Walkman for company. I dined on a truck stop patty melt, bunked at a Holiday Inn, and then the next morning drove through Arizona to California, finally exiting the I-10 at Wilshire Boulevard in Santa Monica at about one thirty a.m.

Keeping it simple, Bryan had said, "Just get off of the I-10 where it dead-ends in Santa Monica, take a right on Wilshire and a left on Orlando; you can't miss it." If you know LA at all, you know that where the I-10 dead-ends into Santa Monica at the Pacific Ocean is a long way from Orlando Avenue in Beverly Hills. Still, I did as I was told and cruised the red Honda east through about fifty-two stoplights, then knocked loudly on the door of apartment B to wake my brother as instructed.

This time, there were no margaritas or wannabe starlets to celebrate my arrival, just my half-awake brother, who pointed to a futon on the living room floor in his one-bedroom apartment. "See you in the morning," Bryan said as he walked back to his bedroom.

When I arrived in California, I had exactly $2,000 in my pocket, and zero idea what was next. As I lay on the futon before falling asleep that night, I wondered how I would survive here, an outcast with no prospects or contacts other than a brother in the film business, which I knew absolutely nothing about.

My first job in Los Angeles was as a barback at the Restaurant Muse on Beverly Boulevard. It was a chic place—high design, wide aquariums, and long lights, with bad art by *emerging* artists on the walls. Everyone who worked there had to wear white jeans and a white shirt. I had never seen a pair of white jeans before. I washed glasses, filled the beer coolers, retrieved whiskey from the storeroom, sliced lemons and limes, and watched a bartender named Joe flirt with dudes, blend whiskey sours, pour martinis, and open large bottles of Sapporo beer.

It was a good gig. I worked only on Friday and Saturday nights. My boss was a guy named Ron, who was one of my brother's closest friends. I cleared about two hundred in cash each night, my rent was free, and my brother had an expense account and treated me to dinner once a week.

The bars in Los Angeles close at one a.m., and after that, normally, I'd meet Bryan and some of his friends at various late-night speakeasies, which either sold liquor illegally or let us bring our own. I was the new kid in town, and also brother to a rising star, so I frequently found myself in conversations with all sorts of upwardly mobile folks, who often only knew about the South from Civil War textbooks. At first it was quaint, their perception of me as exotic—their grinning or confused curiosity. But the more conversations I weathered, the more I felt alone. I once tried to talk earnestly with some twenty-something urbanites about hunting in wetlands, but it was like looking through a telescope from the wrong direction—something beautiful just ended up looking small and warped.

Still, at least the first time around, I tried to walk them through it—describing what it was like to sleep in the woods with no TV and no paved roads, wild animals howling and fighting under a moonlit sky, and alligators and water moccasins in the water all around you. What it was like to get up early, layer your clothes deliberately, maybe drink some wine out of a dead relative's flask, then reflect in perfect solitude as the sun brimmed over the glassy surface of a pond. The flawed beauty of the cane fields shaking with the hum of crickets just before dawn. I think I liked talking about all of it because it brought me back there.

But not one person who listened, lounging on their bar-size daybeds, expressed much empathy for the longings of a hunter. One observer remarked that my recollections reminded him of Hemingway's short story "The Snows of Kilimanjaro"—which was a compliment, to be sure. But I wondered when these metropolitans left their bookshelves and hallways, their three-hour meetings and luncheons, their commodified "promenades," parties, and bars, and actually met the raw edges of a fresh rain.

I walked outside and leaned against the three-story building, stucco riddling my back as I breathed in the city air. I thought if I waited long enough, dew might collect on my skin and remind me how slim the separation of man from the elements can be, even on a night like this. But not even a wind stirred, and the one cricket I managed to distinguish was pressed over by the intermittent roar of wheels overtaking the road. I knew then how far, far I was from home.

Most nights I went home lonely, even when I had a young girl on my arm. And I spent most of those early days wondering about everyone back home—Dad, Mom, my sister and younger brother. Once in a while when I called the house, I would get Tutu on the line, and he'd fill me in on everything. I knew Tutu was muddling through classes, on the very slow path to a degree, and falling deeper and deeper into the horse trade. The Louisiana thoroughbred business was full of simple men who enjoyed long lives without ever having to use algebra. These men and women had strong backs, a good sense of humor, a willingness to work long hours, and little or no need to earn big paychecks. And Tutu fit right in. He had a way with jockeys, stable boys, and owners, but most of all, he had a way with horses. While I didn't share his passion for horses, I would just sit on the line and listen, happy to be talking with someone from home.

Tutu loved breezin'. On Thursdays and Fridays, the day before a big race, he'd arrive at the track before the sun came up; he'd brush the finest south Louisiana thoroughbreds' lower legs down with alcohol, wrap their knees with Ace bandages, and mount up, riding at three-quarter speed till daybreak. He'd found his divinity in nature, too.

And then he met a girl.

Tutu first met Christie on Lingerie Night at Pancho's Bar when she was in town for a friend's wedding. Pancho's had been a Mexican restaurant until some point in the mid-eighties when the owners decided that Mexican food in south Louisiana was a pain in the ass and turned it into a honky-tonk instead. The locals called it "the trailer" because that's what it was: two mobile homes fastened together, side by each. The outside wall of the place was painted with a green cactus and a setting sun to resemble an oasis, and the parking lot was always full of trucks and early-model LTDs.

Christie understood Tutu. She was the third of three daughters, and from the moment he bought her a tequila sunrise at the trailer, they bonded in a sibling kind of kinship and became inseparable. After a few weeks, he introduced her to Mom. Christie was amazed at how alike she and Sherion were. She told Mom that she was in love with her son, and that she hoped they would someday marry. At some point, this piece of news was leaked to Tutu, though he hardly needed prompting.

He also told me about Deb, who had turned to boys in search of a man who would give her the attention Puff never gave her. The first boy she dated was a handsome, lean boy named Kyle, whose father owned a restaurant and a gas station. Kyle was a great athlete. He loved water sports of all kinds, and for reasons unknown, he always had a wallet full of money. Somehow, south Louisiana always seems to get in the way of a young man's promise. It may be the haze layer, the constantly overcast sky, the vacillations from heat to cold, the laissez-faire attitude passed down from generations, the romantic ethic of the gamblers, or maybe it's the learned behavior from the unlived lives of the boys and girls who raise us.

Kyle would pick Deb up most nights in his new gold 1984 Chevy half-ton truck with chrome wheels and straight pipes, and they'd go riding. Deb was pregnant by the end of her senior year, and a small marriage ceremony was held at our oil-boom house on the Bayou Wind Road. I did not attend the ceremony because I wasn't invited. I was prideful and objected to the entire situation, as though it was mine to judge. How could anyone really be happy to see their little sister get pregnant, miss college, and end up living in a motel room? Deb wanted out of the storm, but quickly found herself in another.

Deb's first son was born that spring, and she named him Zane. And in their first year, Kyle was a pretty good husband. He worked seven on, seven off, on an oil rig in the Gulf of Mexico. There is always a need in the oil patch for manual laborers, men who were willing to live alone with thirty other men in the middle of the Gulf of Mexico, eating bad food and risking life and limb. Most people work offshore as a quick way to make money, but some men turn it into a career. For some, the work has a nice rhythm, seven days with the wife and family and seven days offshore hunting oil, "turning it to the right." Kyle never liked being offshore, though—maybe because the work was hard, or maybe because, like most Coonasses, he hated being away from his truck, his Jet Ski, his whiskey, his friends, and his girl.

Mom and Dad never really accepted Kyle, and slowly, Deb found it harder and harder to do so herself. When you're raised by a man who's become a "less-than" thinker, it can be hard to choose a partner who sees and appreciates your strength.

When I got Dad on the phone, he was always short. It's tough to find things to talk about when you're avoiding so many other, bigger things. We'd curtly talk about the local sports teams or the weather, then hang up. He was in the middle rounds of a fifteen-round bout with a deflationary commodity cycle that he would not win and woke up every day hoping that any little rally in the price of oil would stick.

As the months went by and the sleeping arrangements were perfected, my futon was sectioned off from the rest of the living room by a Chinese screen that my big bro acquired at a swap meet in Pasadena. On Monday mornings, after perusing the *Los Angeles Times* classifieds, I would usually stuff about ten résumés, along with personalized cover letters typed on nice paper, into high-quality envelopes and mail them to various securities firms. There were lots of them.

I was careful to always follow the instructions I had received from friends with jobs, recruitment services, and my older brother. Write a good cover letter. Be direct in it. Be clear in your job description. Have goals; goals are important. Use good paper stock on the letter and the résumé. Always, always be early for meetings when you get them.

It was a Friday morning in the summer of 1987 when I finally got the call from a sales manager at E. F. Hutton in Santa Monica inviting me in for an interview.

I arrived promptly at 8:55 a.m. the following Monday. I took a simple math test that a sixth-grader could pass and interviewed with a man named Lou Bird, who was originally from Brooklyn. He had the first set of capped teeth I had ever seen and the belly of a guy who sat around and talked on the phone. He drove a beautiful white 1987 BMW 535 sedan. I was careful to comment on all the personalized trinkets and gimcracks that adorned his office, which overlooked a piss-stained alley behind the Third Street Promenade. I was complimentary when I could be and, overall, bullish. We had a good rapport. Lou liked the social-chairman aspect of my résumé and said that, given my drive and energy, selling securities in Los Angeles would be a walk in the park.

In the end, Lou was the gatekeeper to my dreams of Wall Street riches. I got the call on a Wednesday right after my afternoon nap.

"Blaine Lourd, please," a man said matter-of-factly.

"Speaking," I said, hoping that it wasn't the cops.

"Lou Bird, E. F. Hutton. Blaine . . ."

"Yes, sir."

"Blaine, we got your test scores back."

I held my breath.

"I'm prepared to offer you $1,500 per month as a draw for six months and then it's straight commission. Can you start on Monday?"

"Yes, I can," I said enthusiastically, then added "thank you" and, regrettably, "You won't regret it, Mr. Bird."

I called Bryan first, who was relieved and happy to learn that I would not be considering promotion to bartender at the Restaurant

Muse. I thought of calling my dad but then changed my mind, remembering how miserably we'd left things. It was better to assume he wouldn't share my joy than to call and discover it all over again. What part of what I was aspiring to do might he like? Not one inch of it. Besides, a man controls nothing but his own thoughts, and my dad's thoughts were not good.

My new cubicle at E. F. Hutton was located at 201 Santa Monica Boulevard in Santa Monica, California. "Smile and Dial" was the raison d'etre for stockbrokers in the late eighties. After I was licensed by the federal government, Lou Bird handed me a reverse directory and said, "Smile and dial, boy," with a smirk on his face, then walked back to his corner office. I placed the book on my desk next to a number two lead pencil, a purple highlighter, and an empty Rolodex, waved off the cloud of dandruff Lou had left in his wake, and picked up the receiver with a sigh.

Almost in a matter of days, I learned how to tie a Windsor knot, find stock quotes on the computer, and pitch stocks from a script better written than most Hollywood screenplays. All I had to be able to do was dial a phone, ask strangers to send me money, and hear the word "no" often enough to get to one "yes." On the floor I was the eccentric Southerner, the guy who didn't mind the early mornings, the windows wide open, and rain in the forecast. I kept waiting for some promotion, some new position that would bring me from the level of mountebank to respectability. I did not yet understand that, in the traditional investment banking business, this wasn't only an initiation; this was all there was. There was no more.

From the moment I began cold-calling, I disliked it. But I was determined not to fail. America does not appreciate failures. It did not matter that I had no clue about stocks, bonds, or markets. Cold-calling is the original numbers game. If you dial a phone three hundred times a day, you will talk to fifty people and five of them will be okay with you calling them back. Of those five people, one will consider this, that, or the other thing and give you an order to buy stock. But never does a prospect go down easily. There are always objections.

Most cold calls began and ended with the target's secretary, if she was good. If a stockbroker was lucky enough to get past the secretary, it was usually as a result of some lie, such as "Yes, he's expecting my call" or, even further, "Yes, his wife asked me to call." Even then, the target usually ended the conversation with a quick "I'm not interested" and hung up. A *good* broker would say anything to get to the money.

"Hello, Mr. Johnson, this is Blaine Lourd with E. F. Hutton in Santa Monica. How are you today?"

"How'd you get this number?"

"Mr. Johnson, I'm calling at the request of Governor Deukmejian."

"You're calling at the request of whom?"

"That's right, Mr. Johnson, we are offering, through George Deukmejian and the state legislature's approval, Triple-A, tax-free income in a California Revenue Municipal Bond. Are you currently taking part in any tax-free income?"

"No, actually, I'm not. What's the minimum?"

That was the only opening I needed. His guard was down. The minimum was never really the minimum, but if he didn't buy today, I'd at least get the chance to call him back. I would write all the information down on an index card and file it away to call back in ten or fifteen days. I would then mail him a note on high-quality paper and enclose my business card, which read "Blaine Lourd, Financial Consultant."

Ultimately, over the course of three months, I would find *something* that this guy wanted. There were no appointments, no meetings, and few papers to sign. Just a "yes," and I would be paid handsomely. I never called poor people. Poor people couldn't afford my services. The people most in need of financial counseling can never afford it.

About a year into my informal education, Tutu called me from the track. It had been a tough ride for Tutu. Soon after they'd met, he and Christie had been married in a small civil ceremony, but a lightning storm and fog had stranded me at the airport that day. I'd regretted having to call from the Houston airport to wish him good luck and tell him I loved him. Tutu's reply had been smooth, though; Tutu was always able to tell his brothers that he loved them in an easy, truthful way. He could say it effortlessly at the beginning or at the middle of a conversation, unlike the rest of the Lourd men, who could only say "I love you" just before they hung up the phone.

The hall where the ceremony had been held was owned by his ex–high school teacher Wayne Peltier. Mom and Dad reached deep into what little was left of their savings and gave them $1,000 as a wedding gift. Tutu's friend Bruce had driven in from Baton Rouge in a monster truck, and afterward, they all ate fried shrimp balls. Tutu and Christie went to New Orleans for their honeymoon, stayed at the Orleanian, and ate lobster at the Court of Two Sisters restaurant, just as Mom and Dad had thirty years earlier. Christie had never eaten lobster before.

At first, Tutu and Christie went everywhere together. He was a true and devoted husband, and she was a good wife. Like most children of the oil bust, they always had money problems, but they were happy. She believed in him and thought that things would come together soon enough. Their parents helped whenever they could, but their purse grew more meager every day.

Until one day, Christie left—wrote him a note, and was just gone. Tutu was stunned and forlorn. He grabbed his cigarettes and keys, got in his car, and drove to his sister's house. Deb called me that evening to tell me, and I asked how I could help.

"He ain't saying much," she said.

"Yeah, he never does," I said. If Tutu had secrets, he kept them from us, inviolate, whatever the cost. Tutu trusted few people, but he and Deb could always comfort each other without words. He visited her often during this time to get a meal, to watch sports, or just to be near the one person in his blood family who had no expectations of him.

The truces we keep with ourselves, the oaths we honor, the secrets we withhold from ourselves and others define us.

As I picked up Tutu's call, I could hear the sounds of trainers talking and a horse whinnying in the background as we exchanged preliminary hellos.

"I got a real hot horse here, Blaine. He runs his first race in two days, and I want to claim him," Tutu confided, his voice tight with a familiar intensity.

"Yeah?" I said.

"Yeah. But it'll take about seven hundred to do it." He waited a moment. "What do you say?"

I continued studying the fluctuations on the Quotron, red and green flickering up and down with dogged persistence. My brother was not really so different from our father, in some ways—fervent, mysterious, liked to keep to himself, often taciturn. My brother never admitted to much. I knew it'd taken him a lot to make this call. I knew he needed something, anything, to make him feel good after Christie.

Finally I said, "It's all chance, Tu."

He was quiet. I could hear his breath and someone else in the background.

"I know." He didn't have to say much else. I wanted to give it, even if I didn't have it.

I shifted in my chair. "I can give you three hundred. You'd have to get the rest from someone else," I offered. I could hear the grin rising quickly in his voice as he answered.

"Great, bro. I can get the rest from Pinky. That's great." Three hundred was half my net paycheck, but it was Tu. I looked out the window.

"How's Deb?" I asked.

His voice was easier now. "Oh, you know. She's taking care of her baby and not much else. We all wish she'd leave Kyle," he murmured.

"And Dad?" I finally asked.

"He and Mom hardly say a stitch to each other some days," he replied. "Since you left he hasn't been the same."

I was there on Black Monday, October 19, 1987, when all the screens went red. I was in a conference room on the trading floor, studying stocks and bonds and options and mutual funds to prepare myself for life as a salesman, when the market came crashing down around me. Brokers in the bullpens stared at their screens in fear and confusion. I talked about it with a guy named Ken that day, right before the market closed.

"Ken," I begged, "can I ask you a question?"

Ken lit a cigarette in his cubicle. He looked up at the screen again and sighed. "Sure, Blaine."

"What's going on?" I asked, referring to the red dots on his screen. "What's happening?"

He took a long pull on his Viceroy and, without looking at me, said, very patiently, with a tinge of fear in his voice, "More sellers than buyers, Blaine. More sellers than buyers."

At the time, I was completely oblivious to the fact that billions of dollars that had taken years to accumulate had just vanished in one day's trading. I was oblivious to the fact that there can *never* be more sellers than buyers. I walked back to the conference room, unaware, as was most of the rest of the world, that I was witnessing the equity-buying opportunity of the century. Temporarily gone were the dollars, but back was the vulnerability in the participants—vulnerability that had been artificially allayed since 1982 by ever increasing prices.

A week or so later, I asked one of the biggest producers in the office what he planned to do, assuming, mistakenly, that this business I had chosen was now ruined.

"Well," he said, looking down at his Rolex, "I'm certainly not going to stop making a living. I'll find *something* to sell them."

14

It was six months later when I opened my eyes to the faint ringing of the phone in my LA living room. I lay in bed, listening to the all too familiar pounding in my head after a night of copious amounts of beer, liquor, techno disco, and Virginia Slims menthol cigarettes.

The ringing continued, but I did not answer it, contending as I was with a nagging fear in the pit of my stomach. The sky was annoyingly clear outside, which did not match my head. I regretted being able to see, just by looking, that the Louisiana humidity did not grace the spindly, domesticated trees visible from this stale apartment. And whatever else I chose to look at did not distract me from this fear, which cloaked me like a thick fog.

The fear was of phone calls I had to make. Phone calls that rose up and cascaded over one another like a cacophony of shrill teenage girls all uncertain who they wanted to be but desperate to tell you anyway. Phone calls so prefabricated and prone to exaggeration they could choke a man. Phone calls that wanted to claim me, hold me underwater until I wondered if there was some mistake and I was supposed to be a fish. Phone calls.

That's what my life was. The noonday sun pierced through the shades into my one-bedroom apartment, and I wondered where the little dog that had shit in my mouth had gone. Appearance was everything in California. I was becoming more toxic and lean by the day. I pretended that I wasn't a smoker by never buying cigarettes, and by saying that I only smoked when I drank. The problem was I drank all the time. Everyone told me I looked great, even though I felt like crap. I hadn't eaten anything more than a cocktail rind after six p.m. in a couple of months. The summer was nearly gone, even though, in Los Angeles, it's difficult to tell.

For his part, Bryan still liked working fifteen-hour days; he was well suited to his profession and was promoted to agent at William Morris. Along with his new title, he had a new Alfa Romeo convertible and a closet full of designer clothes. I'd since gotten my own place, and was growing more and more restless in my Santa Monica cubicle. Whenever I met someone who I thought was a player on Wall Street, I told him that rejection was my middle name.

"Rejection? I don't give a damn about rejection. It matters not what anyone says to me on the phone. I cannot be wounded. I've been rejected all my life. I'm the middle child. I've always just wanted to be rich, and I will do anything it takes to reach that goal."

There was only one problem with my pitch. In my heart, I knew it was all a lie. In truth, I did not like rejection. I did not like phoning people at home. I did not like lying to secretaries. I did not like summoning the hubris it takes to get to the top of the heap selling securities, and I especially did not like losing the money of complete strangers.

I was two people: outside, an actor in the role of a Wall Street tycoon who was about to conquer all, but inside, a scared boy who found that the more he got what he thought he needed, the worse he felt.

Finally making it out my front door, I drove the six miles to my office building, said the cursory hellos to those around me, and sat down in front of my Quotron. A pawn in the game, a consumer, I had a car payment, a gold Visa card, and a Beverly Hills apartment.

I had learned how to prey on my customers, but the top layer of my imaginary leather skin was peeling off, and dread was never further from my consciousness than the space between my eyes.

Still, I knew of no other way to get rich.

No matter what hour of the day, invariably, I would have to call yet another prospect to arrogantly beg. And invariably another assistant would answer the phone.

"Will he know why you are calling?"

"He will if he's clairvoyant," I snapped.

There was a pause. I was certain she wore a belly button ring, had a bull's-eye tramp stamp on the small of her back, and hiked Joshua Tree on weekends with an actor named Chase, who had a tribal armband tattoo and was at the very vanguard of organic dining.

"Please hold, sir."

"Just *put him on the phone*, please," I barked. Something in my tone suddenly struck an anxious chord in my gut. Dad's words came back to me: *What happened to you, man?*

"Sorry, sir, he's going to have to call you back."

"Hey, I'm sorry about that outburst. I'm having a bad day," I said, my Southern manners returning.

"It's okay. Try some green tea instead of coffee."

Sometimes at night, I would lie in my bed in silence. I felt as though some beast had replaced all that was good in my life. Often I'd dream that something terrible was happening to me or someone I loved. Sometimes I'd die in my dreams.

At one point, as I sat sorting the fluctuating rhythms on the Quotron, the voice on the other end of my fiftieth phone call turned out to be Mom. I should have been happy, but I wasn't in the mood. As it turns out, it didn't matter what kind of mood I was in.

"Blaine, I have some bad news," she said.

"What?"

"Cecil died."

"Mr. Cecil died?"

"No, Cecil Jr. died."

Tears took my breath away. I sat up in my chair.

"Mom, that's impossible."

"I'm sorry, Blaine."

I flew back to New Iberia for the funeral. As I got off the plane, the lush wind filled my lungs, and the ache around Cecil seemed limitless, but something settled in me. I needed to be here. Maybe fate was bringing me home with good reason. Bringing me home, at twenty-five, for good. The thought surprised me, quickening my step.

I walked into our house and immediately hugged Mom, then found an awkward embrace with Dad. The place looked out of shape, but also the same. Mom talked in a tight voice about Cecil's family, and I heeded her more keenly than usual. I found a respite on the back porch for a moment and, watching the cypresses sway, knew how much I missed Dad.

We took two cars to the service, Dad and I driving alone. The brief phone conversations we'd stumbled through since I'd left for Los Angeles eerily haunted the quiet. But we were protected from speaking about either him or me by the circumstances, a blessing and a curse.

Watching Cecil lowered into his gravesite, I could not help but think that I would fit just as well as he into that rectangular hollowing of earth. Afterward, my mom and I took her car to Cecil's parents' to deliver a casserole in an attempt to console them. Tutu was there, aloof as always. Deb, dressed nicely but with a heavy heart, joined us with her toddler, Zane, and her second baby, Bronwyn.

Deb had tried hard to make her relationship with Kyle work, but like so many things that began in the oil-bust days, they could just never get any traction. She'd left him for a while, but she always went back to him, hoping to keep the family together. Kyle was more of a friend than a father to their kids, though, and he and Deb finally divorced after a two-year separation. Deb then moved out of his family's house and into one of Dad's few remaining rental properties, a small two-bedroom house.

Where a man will run, a woman will stand her ground. In the years since Bryan and I left New Iberia, Deb had spent most of her days raising her children and picking up the pieces of our broken family. The bayou can be hard on its own.

As I looked at Deb, though, I still saw in her that confident agility that girls with brothers possess in abundance. For a minute, I took Bronwyn in my lap.

"She's beautiful. How many months now?"

"Eighteen."

"Thanks for everything you've done for Maw-Maw and Paw-Paw and Mom and Dad while we've been gone."

Deb just nodded, saying nothing.

The faces at the Broussard home were the same faces I'd seen for years—a few cousins of Cecil's who'd driven in from Midland, Texas; some midlevel managers from the AutoMart; and all of Mr. Cecil's and Ms. Bea's tennis friends and business buddies. Of course, all his brothers and sisters were there, talking softly to mourners and trying to process their feelings and the loss.

As Dad and I walked around greeting people, I caught those

sad, dejected looks of shock and impermanence. I didn't turn away. I shook hands with a few of those not in the know—those who weren't close to the family but who'd come to pay their respects anyway. Louisianans are big on paying respects; they always expect a big rainstorm, or the other shoe to drop, and remain ready for the tragedy that is life. After all, they've lived through hurricanes, tornadoes, floods, anything this land could deliver.

All their queries were kind, true, and sympathetic, but as I heard them each trying to comprehend how a twenty-seven-year-old could just die, I realized in that moment that facts don't matter when you're dead. He was dead; no explanation of how or why would help with the facts. I walked around the living room, picked up a finger sandwich from a silver tray, and left Dad talking to Uncle Gary from Midland. I walked through the house, around the guests and to the bar, where Butter Bean, the attendant from the New Iberia Country Club, said, "I'm very sorry, Mr. Blaine . . . I knows how close you and C-Junya was . . ." His eyes were dark and deep, and I could tell he'd been crying, too, as he handed me a Coca-Cola in a large Styrofoam cup branded with purple lettering that said "Cecil and Bea."

"Thanks, Butter Bean . . . I appreciate it."

I walked out of the house through the back door, past the pool, and into the sprawling backyard. I stood under the blue-and-gray sky of the delta and admired the tree swing that was hooked atop a perch we'd built from two-by-fours some years ago. I remembered the hours Cecil, his brother Bart, Tutu, and I had spent climbing, jumping, and swinging out of that tree, before we had motorcycles, girlfriends, and cars. The tree was one of those majestic beauties that the bayou country was full of, though it topped them all; it was spectacular. Easily the biggest and oldest tree in the neighborhood, it was tall, thick, and wild. Having been fed a constant deluge of rain, and sitting atop some of the richest soil in the country, this tree was built to last, unlike many things in Louisiana. Its limbs stretched forty feet wide in every direction, and when the wind blew, it swayed like a giant octopus floating in the ocean. Its trunk was dotted with green algae, and a few mushroom pods had made a home in its moist bark. The Spanish moss that hung from its branches was dark gray and thick, and as I watched a male squirrel run and jump from limb to limb, I started to hum the Jackson Browne song "For a Dancer," which Cecil and I had listened to so many times: "*I don't know what happens when people die, can't seem to grasp it as hard as I try . . .*"

Cecil Jr. had always been larger than life. A Coonass at heart. Like me, he expected to cash in on the high-growth era of the Southern oil states. He was never much of a student but went to LSU, anyway, because he had been born here, and before 1990, if you were born in Louisiana, had a high school diploma, had any ACT score, and could pay tuition, you could go to LSU. Governor Huey Long was a genius.

We used to joke about being part of the idle middle-class elite. Cecil Jr. would pick me up on Friday nights in the Corvette that he'd coaxed his father into buying for him, and drink Dom Pérignon from a bottle on his lap while we cruised the streets. He had smoked cigarettes since he was sixteen—they were always the same brand, Marlboro menthols. He would eat mayo-only cheeseburgers and peanut M&M's as we rode in a big circle from McDonald's on Main Street, down past the clothing boutiques, then by the old hospital, then around the city park and back. After he got his pilot's license, he often said that the best way to go would be to go down in his jet with his mistress as copilot somewhere over the Bermuda Triangle, never to be seen again. That's why I loved Cecil. He lived his life every day like he meant it, with no compromises.

Cecil and I both double dated often in high school, and the girls always had to be home before us, so we mainly had dinner, drove around for three or four hours, and sometimes went to a movie. I could always talk Cecil into dropping off his date first. When our time was up, I'd walk my date quietly over the pebble driveway, past the box hedges to her front door, where we'd make out in the doorway until Cecil gave the signal. Cecil was a good friend. He'd sit in his car listening to a James Taylor eight-track tape for an hour or so while we kissed; then he'd gently begin blowing his horn.

I remember one date in particular. Gail Meeks, the girl I so curtly dumped after Reynosa, was beautiful and smart. As usual, I had walked her to her front door and pulled her over to the side of the house to get a bit more intimate. After a while, Cecil tapped the horn.

"You better go. He's going to wake up my dad," she whispered.

"I'm not worried about your dad; he likes me. It's your mom that I'm worried about."

"My mother thinks you are the Coonass devil, pure and simple," she whispered into my mouth on the second horn blow, which was always about five minutes after the first. A warning bell, if you will.

That was the first time I'd ever felt being a Coonass counted against me. As lost in the moment as I was, I had to know more.

"And what do you think?" I asked.

Our faces were only inches apart, my body tingling from the

smell of her breath and the heat of her heart. She looked at me sideways, eyes shining, and said, "I think you're just sexy."

When I got back to the car, climbing into the thick vinyl passenger seat, Cecil looked over at me and saw the smile on my flushed face.

"You can thank me later for that. I gave you an extra ten minutes."

Still collecting my breath, I said, "Thank you, C. This might be the best night of my life."

"Yeah, why's that?"

"She called me the 'Coonass devil.'"

"Nice." Cecil laughed as we drove off. "What do you want to hear?"

"You pick, C," I said, and rolled down the window. He opened up his cassette box and pulled out Jerry Jeff Walker's *Ridin' High*, and we listened to "Pissin' in the Wind" all the way home. It was one of my favorite songs, too.

In the end, Cecil didn't die in his jet. In fact, his death was an epically cruel twist of fate. The girl who watched him die initially told his parents that he'd died moving a refrigerator. After a year or so, plagued by the guilt of it all, she showed up unannounced at his brother Brad's office, and over a plate of speckled trout and a bowl of seafood gumbo at the Petroleum Club, she finally admitted that Cecil's aorta had, in fact, burst while in orgasm on top of her. The way she recounted it, when he died at climax, she thought he had simply fallen asleep after too much Dom Pérignon. She didn't call the paramedics until it was way too late.

Brad immediately felt better, as did the rest of his family, because, if there was one thing they knew about Cecil Jr., it was that he would *never* have moved a refrigerator.

Leaving the gigantic oak tree, I walked past the edge of the backyard onto the dirt road that bordered the cane field, where the tractors and harvesters wait to enter the fields. I looked over the planting rows that centered the big area between old Loreauville Road and old Jeanerette Road, two paths to smaller towns on the outskirts of New Iberia. I watched some killdeer fly and whistle overhead and admired the meadowlarks as they dipped and dived in a tight covey over the cane field. I thought about how when people pass from our lives, what remains of them is up to us. After the loss and the grief, we choose the pictures we frame for the wall of memories we carry with us until we pass. I would hold him close.

I walked back into the house and hugged Ms. Bea, then shook Mr. Cecil's hand one more time. That's when I spotted Dad by the door; he gave me the wink of "let's go," and I calmly and smoothly followed him out of the door.

15

The feeling of a burial is hard to shake. It was a hot afternoon as Dad and I drove in silence to the Evangeline Downs Racetrack outside Lafayette in the town of Opelousas. This garish prefab metal building was the Cajun version of the grand Churchill Downs racetrack in Louisville, Kentucky, home of the Kentucky Derby.

Dad was drunk. I watched him swagger and sway up to the betting window, money in hand.

"Give me a hundred to win and two hundred to place on the Three horse, and I want a hundred-dollar 3-5-9 exacta box," Puffer said sotto voce to the teller like he was passing along a hot tip on the cure for cancer.

As he spoke, I realized he believed what he said to the teller at the betting window. His best salesmanship was the job he was doing on himself. I'd known for a while that, like most of us, Dad generally tried to figure out what he thought was in his best interests and then rationalized whatever served them. But an assertion cannot be made fact simply by declaring it to be true. I waited, but we said nothing further of Cecil.

On any given day, Puffer was the master of his own redemption or the victim of a cruel twist of fate, depending on which horse came in first. Within an hour I saw how he paid for his splendor with cyclic defeat. And he had a temper to back it up. I've been told that, at its core, a bad temper is symptomatic of self-loathing.

The impassive teller punched in his bet and handed him the tickets. He checked them and slipped them into his shirt pocket, spilling beer on a few shoes in the line as he stumbled over to me. In Louisiana, a little beer on the shoes is a good thing.

We made our way back to his table in the clubhouse of Evangeline Downs. Red greeted us as we sat down. I liked Red a lot. He was a man who could make a gumbo for two hundred people on an hour's notice and knew every racist and sexist joke ever told. I took a gulp of Red's beer as he rubbed my shoulders in recognition of Cecil's death. I'd had enough of death, tears, and eternal salvation for one day, so I drank quickly to fill the hole and catch up with the party.

"Puff, you bet the Three horse?" Red asked him, pulling his hand from my neck apologetically.

"Nah, I don't think he can beat the Eight horse," Dad said.

"I thought you were high on the Three horse," Red said.

Dad leered at him, irritated, discreetly folded his racing form and put it in his back pocket, then took a swig of his beer and began counting his money under the table. Red looked to me for a response, but I said nothing. Lisa, the beer maid, came by.

"You ready for another one?" she asked Puff.

"Yeah, and bring Red and my son one, too."

He handed her a five-dollar bill. She slipped it into her ample cleavage and blew him a kiss, but he didn't even notice her as he continued nervously counting his money under the table. Red whistled at her as she walked by. She glanced back and flipped up her skirt to taunt him. The announcer came over the PA.

"Two minutes to post. Two minutes to post."

Red got up and hurried off to place his bet on the Eight horse. A few minutes later, Poog, an ex-jockey, joined us at the table as Red was coming back with his tickets for the ninth race.

"Poog, where you been?" Red asked. Dad looked up to listen.

"Ah been down at dah paddock talkin' to Tutu. I tell you wha, baw, that fuckin' Three hoss looks good," Poog replied.

"Of course it looks good," Dad said. "That's why it's paying three-to-two. It's the favorite! I used to own that horse."

"Yeah," I said. "We used to own that horse. That's News Brief."

"What did Tutu say?" Dad asked Poog.

Tutu was down in the stables, a trainer's apprentice at this time. He liked it better down there; he appreciated that the only thing horses wanted was a good mount and a good meal.

"Ah, you know, he likes the Nine hoss. He says it's due," Poog answered, cockily unaware of his own foolishness.

Dad disagreed. "Last time out, that horse was leading by six lengths into the eighth pole when he threw the fuckin' jockey. Horse won by ten with no jockey. I don't think that horse can hold a rider."

Lisa brought back a tray of drinks just as the announcer's voice boomed over the PA. "The horses have reached the starting gate."

Silence came over the track. The bell rang. The announcer continued, "*Il sont partir!*"

We stood on our feet, me quickly and Red and Dad slowly, as did most of the patrons at Evangeline Downs. Dad had one hand on his beer and the other one in his pocket, nervously clutching his money as the announcer continued.

"And it's Number Three, News Brief, with a great start taking the inside rail by a head, followed closely by the Number Two horse, Silky Lady. Close behind is the big gray horse, Number Nine, New York Folly. They're at the first turn and News Brief is ahead by two lengths. Closing in on the outside is the Six horse, Crystal Blue Persuasion."

Poog stamped his feet. "Goddamn it, I knew I shoulda bet that Six horse."

Puff and Red glared at the premature Monday morning quarterback and then quickly fixed their eyes back on the herd of horses that were running toward us in a cloud of low-flying dust. The announcer continued, "They're at the halfway point, and it's News Brief by two lengths, and closing into third is the Five horse, The General, followed by the Nine horse, New York Folly, and in fourth is the Eight horse, Hard Left, coming strong."

Dad stared at the Eight horse in bewilderment, put his hand on my shoulder, and whispered under his breath so only I could hear him, "Go, Three . . . Go, Three . . . Go, Three . . ."

Red had his ticket in hand, and clearly, he had bet on the Eight horse. He was chanting aloud, "Come on, Eight, Mama needs a new pair of shoes. Come on, Eight, Daddy needs an oil change down at the Chez Paris."

I watched Poog light another cigarette, lean over, and steal a sip of Red's fresh draft beer, then slide it back into place just as Red reached over to pick up the cup.

The announcer continued, "We're at the sixteenth pole, and it's News Brief by three lengths. In second, the Five horse, The General, and it's the Nine horse, New York Folly, and the Eight horse, Hard Left, in a dead heat for third. The horses are in the stretch and they're coming to the wire. And it's going to be the Three horse, News Brief, by about five lengths. And it's News Brief, your winner, ridden by Jorge Martinez, followed by the Number Five horse, The General, in second, and Hard Left, with the Number Eight horse in third."

The crowd sighed as the announcer repeated the call. Red crumpled his ticket stub and threw it on the table. Poog began his usual postrace commentary. Dad sat down gingerly and stared over the top of his glasses at the form to study the lineup for the ninth race.

I chugged more beer as I looked over my racing form. Dad tossed his winning ticket and fifty dollars down on the table in front of me and said, "Go cash this in and bet me one thousand dollars to win on the Eight horse for the ninth. And get us a couple more beers." Red looked at the ticket in disbelief, and then up at Puff.

"I thought you bet the Eight horse, Puff."

"I did, but I had a little side on the Three as my insurance policy."

"Well, I'm a monkey's fuckin' uncle, Puff. You always holdin' out on me," Red cried.

"Red, I can't tell you all my secrets," Dad said. He winked at me and leaned his chair back on two legs, basking in his handicapping acumen. Red looked to me for a reaction. I could only shrug, for, as a Southerner with manners, I was not inclined to outwardly judge my dad's clandestine arrangements.

Dad grabbed his beer, pinky outstretched, took a long, slow sip, and let out a loud, bellowing, *refreshed* sound, smug in his glory as the man of the moment.

Lisa shimmied over to the table and plopped down in a chair next to him. "You winnin', Puff?" she asked.

"Always winnin', baby," Puff said, staring at the post board on the infield.

"You winnin', Red?" she asked sarcastically, already knowing the answer.

"Always *not* winnin', baby," Red said, shaking his head.

"I'm getting off at the top of the tenth," Lisa said. "You guys going to the Turf Club after this?"

"I don't know," Dad replied. "I may rent a jet and fly to Vegas for the night."

Red looked over at Lisa. "Lisa, I'll go wichya to the Turf Club."

"Red," she said, leaning over to rub Dad's back, "you couldn't find it in a fire."

Dad spit out a bit of beer and let out a drunken guffaw. I forced a fake laugh, too, not liking the rasp of it in my throat.

"Shit, that's not what your daughter says, Lisa," Red snarled.

"Yeah, you wish, Red," Lisa answered, peeved.

"What you women don't understand," Red exclaimed, grabbing his belly and shaking it so that his man tits jiggled broadly, "is that all of this is Cinderella fat. At midnight, it all turns into dick!" Everyone laughed and looked to Puffer for approval.

The PA blared. "Ladies and gentlemen, we are nearing post for the ninth race, the John Thibodeaux forty-thousand-dollar added handicap. Ten minutes till post."

Feeling no pain, I got up and headed for the betting window, where I accidentally stepped in front of a large black woman who was carrying a strawberry daiquiri in one hand and two dollars in the other.

"Excuse me, ma'am; after you, please," I said as I backed away from her.

"No, please; you first," she said as she, too, stepped back. I moved ahead of her as the announcer called, "Two minutes to post. Two minutes to post."

"This must be the slow line," I said to her.

"That's all right, sugar. That means I'll hold on to my money a little longer!" she said, looking down at her two George Washingtons one more time.

I came back a few minutes later with another round of beers

and handed Dad his tickets and the change. He slipped the money into the front pocket of his Wrangler jeans and the ticket into his front shirt pocket. He did that every time. That was his system.

Lisa leaned in closer to Dad, forcing a sweet view of her cleavage on him.

"Red," she said flirtatiously, "you know what I want?"

"Yeah," said Red from across the table as he lit another one of Poog's cigarettes, "and I know what he wants—the fuckin' Eight horse!"

Dad looked over at me, his eyes squinting blue and crimson red, proud that I was there to witness his status.

"Come on, Eight horse," Lisa crooned. "Come to Mama so we can fly to Vegas on a jet." Lisa had never been farther than Houston, and that was by car.

The PA boomed back on. "Ladies and gentlemen, we've got a jockey change for the ninth race. Jorge Martinez will be up, riding the Eight horse, replacing Adam Jones. That's a jockey change on King's Ransom, the Eight horse, with Jorge Martinez now up for Adam Jones."

The crowd scuffled about a bit and then returned to its prerace chatter. Poog slapped his hand on the table.

"Muthafucka, Puff, you got to be the luckiest Coonass alive. If I'd a bet dat hoss, day'd a put Red on that muthafucka!"

We all burst out laughing. Dad leaned back in his chair, feeling ten feet tall and bulletproof. He wrapped his hands behind his head and announced, "I'm going to take a leak, and then get down big on this race."

I watched my father as he got up from the table and walked away as slowly as a seventy-year-old man, even though he was forty-nine, his knees worn out from arthritis and baseball. He seemed strangely frail. I had never seen him in that light before. I felt a sense of foreboding. Poog hurried after him. When he caught up, the two of them huddled close and began to whisper in serious tones.

"Puff," I heard Poog ask, "wha'cha wanna do?"

I saw Dad reach into his pocket. He pulled out a wad of cash and grabbed Poog affectionately in a semiheadlock.

"Here's eight grand," he said. "I want six thousand on the Eight to win, and I want a two thousand 8-2-10 exacta box. The fuckin' Eight is the lock of the year at four-to-one."

I could not believe what I was seeing. Neither could Poog, apparently, because he kept staring down at the money in his hand.

"The lock of the year? Jesus Christ, Puff, I never had this much money in mah hand."

My interest grew as I watched him growing louder and more emphatic.

"The fuckin' lock of the century! Here's the deal, Poog. Jorge Martinez has two hundred ninety-nine wins. They want him to get three hundred wins tonight, so I'm sure he's made some kind of jockey bullshit arrangement with Adam, maybe like splitting the purse or something, because Jorge knows the Eight can't be beat! It's the fuckin' Eight horse! Repeat my bet!"

Poog held Dad's eight grand in a death grip, took a last sip of his beer, and let go of the cup. Not a drop flew as it hit the floor, not even backwash. Every drop of that Bud was in the four-foot-two bad jockey's throat. "Okay, Puff," Poog said. "You want six G's to win on the Eight hoss, King's Ransom, and a two thousand 8-2-10 exacta box. Dat it?"

"That's it. You got it and don't tell a fucking soul what I bet."

He slapped Poog on the back and staggered into the men's room as Poog took off for the cashier.

I grew up understanding that sometimes you win and sometimes you lose, and I have always admired the courage it takes to bet big. Still, I wondered why on earth one jockey would care whether another jockey rounded off his stats on that particular day. At the same time, I curiously felt a slightly envious twinge, and pictured myself placing that $8,000 *lock of the century* bet at the window for my dad.

The announcer's voice blared over the PA.

"Five minutes till post. Five minutes till post."

By the time Dad and Poog got back to the table, the ninth race had begun. By the eighth pole, everything was beginning to unravel, with Number Three, Evolution Monkey, ahead by six lengths. Red was already ripping up his ticket for the ninth race. Dad was on his feet, visibly upset.

"Goddamn it, Lisa," he snapped. "Why don't you make yourself useful and get me a fucking drink!"

"Uh-oh, here we go again," she said and stood up from the table with her hand out. Dad handed her a twenty-dollar bill. She smiled over in my direction as she left.

In the end, the official call was the Number Three horse, Evolution Monkey, finishing first by six lengths, followed by horse Number Two, Herd Mentality, in second; Number Ten, Juncti Juvant, in third place; and King's Ransom, the Number Eight horse, in fourth. No one heard the rest because none of it mattered.

Poog leaned in close to Dad. "Where'd dat fucking Three hoss come from?"

Dad didn't say a word. He stared down at the stats on the

Number Three horse that were printed on the map to the poor-house.

"I'm out of here," Red said. "I've got just enough money left to buy a pack of cigarettes on the way home."

"*Now* you gonna buy cigarettes?" Poog asked him, incredulous, as Red lumbered out of the clubhouse toward the elevator.

Dad stared down at the racing form for a long time, his eyes darting back and forth from the Three horse to the Eight horse. Finally, he muttered to himself in utter sullen disgust, "Goddamn it! I had to go big on the fucking Eight!"

I was suddenly very glad that Poog and not I had been the one to place that bet. Poog got up and scurried off, leaving Dad and me sitting there alone in silence. Finally, without making eye contact, he slid his racing form under his arm, downed his last sip of beer, stood up, and simply said, "Let's go."

I followed him through the clubhouse toward the elevator. Many in the crowd knew Dad as an everyday player and greeted him by name as we walked through. A fat guy wearing Sansabelt pants was standing at the betting window with his wife, who had on a Tabasco-spattered T-shirt. They called to my dad.

"How'd you do, Puff?"

"Smoked 'em in the ninth," Dad lied to them, his head and shoulders pulling upright as he spoke. The fat guy and his wife both grinned as they headed off toward the track. Dad's eyes were fixed on the ground a foot or so in front of his gator-skin boots as we stumbled through the crowd.

As we entered the elevator to go the one floor down from the clubhouse to the parking lot, an elderly woman leaning against the wall of the elevator wearing a faux-rattlesnake fanny pack greeted us. I noticed her admiring Dad's rodeo belt buckle.

"How'd you do?" she asked as he pressed the dimly lit down arrow.

"Smoked 'em in the ninth, and now I'm out of here," he answered, charming in his grandiosity, even when feigned.

The woman responded nonchalantly, "I *got smoked* in the ninth, and now *I'm* out of here."

Their laughter was brief and forced. Puff chivalrously held the doors open for her and bowed as she exited.

"Thank you," she said, flattered, as she walked toward the beer-stained entrance of Evangeline Downs.

"No problem, ma'am. Have a good day," he called out to her.

Puff's glasses fogged as the Louisiana humidity hit him like a blast furnace in the face. He stood for a minute, swaying on his aching legs until his glasses cleared, then began his semistagger through the parking lot to his 1985 powder blue Mercury Sable, looking back only briefly in the direction of the low roar coming from the track.

He unlocked the car, tossed his racing form on the seat, and got in. It was only then that I realized that this was the first Mercury he'd owned since 1976. No more luxury Lincoln Continentals.

The pungent smell of spent chewing tobacco hit me as I sat down in the passenger seat. Dad inserted the key, shifted into reverse, and slowly began to back out. As he did, his right front fender scraped the car to his right. His reflexes slowed from seven or eight beers, he pumped the brakes in slow motion, shifted into drive, pulled the car up a bit, and backed out again, completely oblivious to the scratch he'd made on the blue Dodge minivan unfortunate enough to have been parked next to the Skoal-mobile.

We eased onto the feeder road that bordered the racetrack. Dad fumbled with the floor mat as a semi whipped past the Mercury with its horn at full blast. Startled and angry, he laid on the horn and yelled, "Fuck you, asshole!" as he pushed his car to forty-five miles per hour and tried to steady the vehicle through the back draft as he headed into the Louisiana sunset. Then, in a lowered breath, the self-punishment began.

"Motherfucker! You stupid son of a bitch!"

He glanced down and tuned the AM radio to K-TRAC to catch the last race, and I scooted closer to my door.

"Jesus H. Christ, you had to fucking play it all on the Eight. Brought the fuckin' odds down to three-to-one and the fucker still ran fourth. What do you got now? Fucking one hundred bucks in your pocket, dumb asshole! Shoulda played the fucking Three horse. Shoulda spread him across the board. Goddamn it!"

I knew better than to say anything to him during these periods of retrospective distortion. As I listened to him rationalize randomness, I recognized that gamblers are not genetically engineered to be rational.

We drove home from the track in silence, winding through the country roads in the dark, listening to the sound of gravel crunching under the tires. When we got home we made our way into the kitchen to greet my mom, who was standing at the stove in a pink-and-blue warm-up suit, cooking round steaks over a yellow electric skillet. I hugged her.

"Hey," Dad said without looking at her as he walked through the kitchen door.

"How you doing?" she asked, but she caught only his back as he barked, "Me? I never had a bad day," and continued through the kitchen to the living room bar.

Mom's smile quickly left her face. She looked down and began punching the overdone meat with a fork. I got up from the bar stool and began to pace back and forth.

"Are you all right?" she asked.

"Yes, I think so," I said, and went into the living room to check on him. He held a half-empty drink in his hands as he opened the doors to the bar. He mixed another three-fingered bourbon and water. I watched as he shut the cheaply hinged bar doors, glass in hand, and, without looking up at me, walked the fifteen paces back into the kitchen, where he pulled up the stool closest to the door, took the racing form out of his back pocket, and tightened his grip around his Jack Daniel's and water.

I sat down next to him. Mom glanced up from the burned steaks in the skillet. "How'd you do?" she asked, falsely enthusiastic.

I anxiously awaited his response and thought of the lady at the track for whom he had held open the elevator door. How nice he'd been to her. He hesitated for a beat, took a slow, deliberate sip of his drink, and replied, "I think I won about a thousand."

I looked to Mom to gauge her reaction. She studied the over-cooked round steak, unplugged the skillet, and responded in mock belief, "Oh, that's good. You hungry?"

Dad inspected the round steak and felt around for the lone hundred-dollar bill in his jeans pocket.

"Nah, I'll pass. I had a ham sandwich at the track."

Mom flipped the steak once more unnecessarily.

"Did you see Tutu?" she asked.

"Nah, he didn't come up to the clubhouse. He stayed down at the paddock. Boy loves the smell of horse shit." Puff grunted.

"Well, he gets it honest," she said, defending my younger brother.

"Goddamn! You sound just like my mother. Fucking cook like her, too," Puff said.

"Uh-huh," Mom said, numb to the drunk. "How about Red? Did you see Red?"

"Sure, he lost all his money by the sixth race; had to go home. Poor bastard was as red as a beet."

Mom moved away from the stove, opened a cabinet, grabbed a plate, plopped the round steak onto it, and set it down on the countertop. Dad stared at it drunkenly. She then dropped the skillet into the sink, where it hit the dishwater with a hiss. She turned on the faucet, swiped a Brillo pad across the grease once, turned off the faucet, and turned back to Dad.

"Pat is having a party tomorrow night. Do you want to go?" she asked, knowing the answer.

I looked at him, hoping he'd say yes.

"We'll see," he said. "I'm going to finish my drink and go to bed. Got to go to work early tomorrow. Got to find out the results of the sand report on that well we're drilling in the Lacassine refuge."

Without saying another word to either of us, he took one last pull of his drink, poured the ice into the drain, grabbed his racing form and car keys, and stumbled past Mom, out of the kitchen. I listened to his gator-skin boots scuffle across the faux-brick floor on their way to the bedroom.

"Looks good, Mom," I said. "I'll have some."

Mom picked up the steak, poured a quarter can of pinto beans over it, cracked open a Dr Pepper, and sat down on the stool to eat.

"Help yourself," she said. She set her fork down on the Formica countertop and stared pensively through the bay window, across the backyard toward the bayou. I pulled a beer out of the refrigerator, sat down next to her, and began scraping the beans off the charred surface of the steak. She glanced at the beer, at the beans, at me, then back out the window, saying nothing.

And it was in that moment that I knew it was over between them. She had that faraway look that you can never fully return from. Their mutual disappointments had led to permanent resentments that would never go away. Serenity is inversely related to expectations, and it's much easier going up than it is going down.

16

For me, mornings in Louisiana have always been worth getting up early for. It's the color of the sky that gets you, like mornings at sea where the colors spread out wide across the big canvas. On this morning it was spectacular. I drove with my father in silence, lost in the shifting clouds, the cane along the road as still as a corpse. Other than a few farmers working the fields and a few early-morning delivery trucks en route to or from the Sugar Oaks Country Club, the roads were wide open, and we rolled past the old-money homes that border the sewage-filled Bayou Teche, with Dad occasionally spitting into his McDonald's cup of Skoal-drenched tissue.

It was eight a.m. by the time we pulled into the parking lot of the red-brick building that L&M Specialties shared with an insurance agency. As we walked inside, Ben Dugas, Dad's right-hand man, was already at his desk. We could hear him on the phone in his office, and we stopped in his doorway. Ben nodded and signaled to us with a finger in the air to indicate be quiet, then pointed at the penis-colored rotary dial phone on his desk and pressed the speakerphone button. The voice on the other end sounded anxious.

"Ben, Pat Boudreaux. I'm calling from my house. This is damned important. Is Puff around?"

"Mornin', Pat, I'm not sure. He might have had an appointment this morning. Hold on a second and I'll check." Ben pressed the hold button, gently placed the unlit cigar he had been chewing in the ashtray next to him, crossed his arms, and greeted us with a warm smile.

"Puff, it's your best friend, the banker. You want to talk to him?"

Puff shook his head as he stared at the back wall of Ben's office.

"Ben, tell him I had to go to the rig site and that I'll call him later today or first thing Monday morning."

Ben was a staunch Catholic who did not like the white lies he was roped into telling in the twilight hours of L&M Specialties. He picked up the phone again.

"Pat, I'm sorry, I couldn't catch him. I'll let him know that you called," he said, hoping that would end the conversation. Dad lingered in the doorway, nervously awaiting the response of the vice president and loan portfolio manager of New Iberia Savings and Loan.

"Ben, I'm starting to get that anxious-banker feeling that the guy who's into me for eight hundred grand is avoiding my calls. That wouldn't, that *couldn't* be the case now, could it?" Pat asked.

"Pat, as soon we know something, you will be hearing from us. We just don't know anything more today than we knew at three o'clock yesterday when you called," Ben said calmly.

"Goddamn it, Ben, someone better know something fast, because the board of directors is crawling up my ass on these oil loans. What's up with the well that was the—wait . . . what did Puff call it—the lock of the century?"

"Listen, Pat," Ben said, his lips parting in a slight smile. "We haven't tested it yet, but we should know something tomorrow."

We could hear the banker's number two lead pencil banging on some metal piece of furniture over the phone.

"Ben, just please have him call me. I have to tell the board something."

"Okay, Pat, I'll sure tell him," Ben replied in that cheerful, good-old-Southern-boy way. "Have a good weekend." Ben flipped off the speaker, hung up the phone gently, kicked back in his chair, picked up his cigar, wrapped his arms around his head, and stared back at Dad, skeptically amused. Dad stood in the doorway, gazing down at his $600 ostrich-skin cowboy boots, shaking his head.

"How you doing, Blaine?" Ben asked.

"I'm fine, Mr. Ben, thank you for asking," I said.

"That motherfucker, fair-weather, front-running son of a bitch," Dad said. "I built that fucking bank with all the fucking interest I paid. Fuck him . . . button-down-wearing, two-over-prime cock-sucker."

"Puff, you need to call the man," Ben said, completely relaxed and indifferent to Dad's profane rage, then went back to studying his topographic map highlighted in yellow, pink, and blue. Dad headed to his office without saying another word.

"Oh, hey, Puff, I almost forgot," Ben said, calling out. Dad leaned back into the doorway. "They lost a bit in the hole of the Lacassine well. They're going to have to wait until morning to test."

"Christ," Dad sighed.

Ben stared at his beer gut, bit down on his cigar, and went back to studying the map.

"What else is going on?" Dad asked him.

"Nothing," Ben answered without looking up. "Slower than a snails' race, Puff."

Dad walked the four steps back to his office. I followed him and sat down in a worn leather chair facing his desk. I surveyed the room that I once had hoped to share with him. It looked neglected and unkempt. Three oxidized metal file cabinets lined the otherwise barren wall to my left, and on the back wall was a single oak credenza. To my right was a metal secretary's hutch with an old typewriter. Behind me was a framed photo of Dad standing in the winner's circle at Delta Downs with Tutu and his prized colt, News Brief. Dad's large L-shaped mahogany desk stood in the center of the room, empty except for an oversized Rolodex and a small stack of papers. Behind it, hanging crooked on the back wall, were a couple of duck prints for which he had paid too much while drunk at a Ducks Unlimited dinner one evening. On the credenza, below the prints, were a couple of in-boxes, a bronze drilling derrick sculpture, and a family portrait from the early seventies.

I was struck by the sight of Mom and Dad as they were, back when things were good between them. I studied Bryan's broad smile; Tutu shy, athletic, handsome. Lastly, my sister, Deb, so cute in her Pee Wee cheerleading outfit, born into optimism, not yet affected by the disintegration of dreams.

"This fuckin' well is going to drive me to drink," Dad sighed in frustration, shaking his head. Then he sat up straight in his chair, pulled the Rolodex over, and flipped open the plastic cover. For a moment, the old optimistic determination came back into his eyes and he looked as though he had resolved to end the recession in the oil business all by himself. "This downward slide is going to end," I imagined him saying. His face grew stern as he began flipping confidently through it, one hand on the receiver and the other on the phone, preparing to dial.

Ultimately, Dad flipped through the entire Rolodex, front to back, slowly slumping down farther and farther into his chair— until he came back to the beginning, then closed the lid and, again, hung up the phone.

I pretended to be reading the *Sports Illustrated* I had picked up from Ben's desk. Dad opened the right-hand desk drawer, pushed aside a stack of bills, and pulled out the corporate checkbook. He flipped to the general ledger and checked the balance, shaking his head in bewilderment. He ripped a blank check out of the book, and wrote "ENTERTAINMENT" methodically on the memo line of the check in big block letters, slipped the check into the front right pocket of his blue cowboy shirt with the fake pearl buttons, and got up from the desk. The phone rang again.

"Ben, goddamn it, where the hell is Marge?" he screamed, startling me. "The answering service stops answering the phone at eight a.m. Shit."

"I'll pick it up," Ben called out from the other room.

It was 8:46 a.m. when the chimes at the back entrance of L&M Specialties headquarters finally clanged and Marge, their executive secretary, strolled into the building. Marge was about thirty-two years old and as country Cajun as they come. Her hair was tinted a strange brownish red from too many home dye jobs. She was late, as usual, as she came prancing past Ben's office, smelling like the perfume counter at a Dallas department store. She wore a skintight black T-shirt studded with a rhinestone parrot, a short white skirt that flared like an umbrella at midthigh, and a pair of fancy black roping boots.

"Hey, Ben," she said in her usual jovial tone.

"Hey, Marge," Ben answered from his office.

Marge landed in the doorway of Dad's office, one hand on her hip, and greeted him in a high-pitched Louisiana twang.

"Hey, Puff, what's going on? Nice to see you again, Blaine," she added, suggestively.

"What's going on, Marge, is I'm seriously thinking of starting to dock your pay for every phone call I got to answer because you're late. That's what's going on," he said without looking up at her.

Marge shifted her hips and said, somewhat apologetically, "Ah, Puff, take a chill pill, will ya? It ain't rocket surgery, you know."

Dad looked up at Marge and started to say something, but bit his lip instead as he sat there, staring at her 36-26-36 red-hot white-trash figure.

Marge grinned. He pushed his chair back and began tapping his head against the mahogany desk, mumbling softly, "God, God, God" or "Fuck, Fuck, Fuck"—I wasn't sure which.

Marge came over and grabbed his empty coffee cup from the desk, oblivious to the two-over-prime cocksucker who sat in a big leather chair inside Puff's head all day. "Would you like a cup a coffee, too, sweetheart?" she asked me.

"No, thank you, Marge, I'm fine," I replied.

"All right then," she said, but then changed course in midstream. She set the cup down again, strutted over behind Dad's desk, and started gently massaging his shoulders. Fearless in life and certainly fearless in her position at L&M Specialties, she rubbed her ample breasts against his back as he stretched his neck from side to side. Her hands moved from his neck and shoulders down the base of his spine, briefly violating the back of his pants below his three-inch-thick white belt. Sweetly, softly, she whispered in his ear. "Come on, Puff, it's going to be all right. You know it always is. You want some coffee?"

Dad did not respond. He just hit his head on the desk in frustration again and began to chuckle. "What can I do?" he asked, looking up at me, demoralized and powerless against the forces that had befallen him.

"I always know how to make you feel better, don't I, Puff?" Marge snickered.

"Yeah, Marge, you do," Dad answered reluctantly. Suddenly,

he bolted upright and began to feel around in the pocket of his starched Wrangler jeans for the lone hundred-dollar bill, then moved quickly to his shirt to make sure the blank check was still in his pocket. Marge abruptly stopped rubbing his back and walked into her office.

"I think she's stealing from me," my dad said to me in a low whisper. I looked at him for a moment to see if he was being serious. He was. I'd known Marge almost all my life and knew there was no way she was stealing anything. But I also knew enough about my dad to know when he wasn't asking for a second opinion.

When I was thirteen, Dad took me out hunting woodcock in the bottomland near the bayou on a wet, rainy November afternoon. We were walking with our hunting dog, Deppa, a few yards ahead of us, leading the way. At some point, Dad leaned in closer to me as if to share a confidence, the way a father sometimes does when he wants to tell a son he's proud of the way he handled himself at the club or stood up to another dad's son at a barbecue. I leaned in to hear what he had to say. He whispered, "You boys been fuckin' that dog?"

"No!" I responded in shocked disbelief. I was puzzled as to why he was whispering, since there was no one around to hear.

"Are you crazy?" I asked him. "*You boys,*" I believed, was a reference to Tutu and me.

"Don't act shocked, and don't you *ever* ask me if I'm crazy!" he said. "You wouldn't be the first boy to play with a dog's pussy. Look me in the eye! That dog's been acting funny lately." His voice trailed off as he noticed a pair of mourning doves, which were not in season, flying overhead.

I glanced down at Deppa's backside and answered again, emphatically, "No, Dad, nobody's been fuckin' the dog!"

A pair of woodcocks fluttered up from the cane field, heading for their roost near the bayou. I raised my gun to my shoulder, eyed the bird on the left, and shot once, glad that providence had presented me with a spontaneous change of topic. I was momentarily blinded by the setting sun and then shot again. One of the birds dropped like a stone. Deppa crawled under the barbed wire fence to make the retrieval. Oddly, Dad never raised his gun to his shoulder. He just yelled, "Dead bird," and watched the dog snort around for blood.

Marge returned, her black boots scuffling along the floor, and dropped off a cup of coffee, then went back to her office. Dad stared at her ass as she walked away. So did I.

"Have a good day, Marge," I said as she began to move to the next room.

"Me?" she said, looking back over her shoulder. "I *never* had a bad day."

"I've got to take off, Dad," I said. "Got to catch my flight. Are you going to be okay?"

"Damn," he said, ignoring my concern, because fathers can't risk appearing weak in front of their sons. "Well, she's definitely stealing clothes from Mrs. Porter Wagoner's closet. That fucking parrot shirt is the worst thing I've ever seen," he said. I nodded in agreement and got up to shake his hand.

"'Bye, Dad. I'll see you in the fall for hunting season, okay?"

"Yeah, son, that'd be good," he said, flipping one more time through his Rolodex. Dad sat back and began shuffling his papers in the worldwide headquarters of L&M Specialties.

It was hard to look at him, or any of it, as I walked out. I knew I would not be back in the fall for hunting season. I might not be back, in the real sense, at all.

The cab was waiting for me when I got out of the building. I nodded to the driver, who watched me throw my bags in the trunk and get in.

"Y'all headed to the airport, that right?" the driver asked with a thick Louisiana accent.

"Yeah, gotta be there in twenty," I said, resting my head against the back of the seat and closing my eyes. As the car picked up speed I studied the paint-chipped shutters on the Main Street storefronts, and caught the long faces of a few older men walking from the sports center, where a busted-out window had been patched up with plywood. The marquee on top of the building hadn't been updated for a few years. The men looked at me flatly as our cab passed.

We drove past the sugarcane fields and the country club. When we came to the sign for Spanish Lake, I told the driver to pull in.

"What about your plane?" he asked.

"The plane can wait."

I got out of the car and walked down to the water's edge, where I'd spent so many early mornings with my dad as a kid. As the tadpoles swam and baby bream darted in and out of the duckweeds, I found myself thinking of one day in particular—June 21, 1970, the first day of summer and the longest day of the year. It was six a.m., and we were driving along to Janis on the radio.

Stores open real early in the summertime in Louisiana because men shop for bait, beer, ice, and cold cuts to take on their fishing trips. The early-model VW bus was our second car and was not very dependable, but my brothers and I sure did like it. It had three rows of seats and a bad green-and-white paint job.

"No budget today, son," he said, standing outside the VW bus with a small wad of fives and ones in his hand. "It's your birthday. Whatever you want to drink, you can have. What will it be?"

"Dad, can you get two six-packs of Schlitz?" I asked. He laughed a bit and said, "Yes, I'll get that for me, but what would you like?"

"I'll take three red pops and three orange pops, Dad."

"You got it, son," he said, shutting the car door. I watched him walk through the open doors of the market, singing, "*Busted flat in Baton Rouge, waiting for a train . . .*"

The night before, I'd been so excited to go fishing that I went into his closet and combined all the gear in his freshwater tackle box with the gear in his saltwater tackle box, to be sure we'd have everything we needed for the next day. At the time, Dad kept all his fishing gear, guns, hip boots, and shotgun shells next to his two pairs of dress shoes in his private "sports" closet. This was his sacred place. He didn't have a library. I had been warned in the past about respecting his things, and especially about the sacred place.

I sat cross-legged near the only air conditioner in our midcentury tract home, and studied the multicolored lures, hooks, and worms, daydreaming of the huge fish we'd soon catch. I was clueless to the fact that the freshwater fish we'd be stalking the next day would not bite on saltwater tackle.

When Dad caught me in his closet, he yelled at me loudly for messing with his stuff. In the moment, I paled, holding myself tight. Later, understanding my enthusiasm, he explained the difference between saltwater and freshwater, and apologized for hurting my feelings.

On that first morning of summer and that longest day of the year, I turned that radio up loud and hummed along as I watched Dad come out of the IGA and grab a big bag of ice from the white container that sat outside the store. The honor system was still in effect, and the icebox was not padlocked at night. I watched him pour the ice on the beer and sodas, then hop back in the bus, light a cigarette, grind the old hippie wagon into second gear, and drive us onward. In just a few minutes we were turning in to the drive on Spanish Lake and pulling short, then walking a ways on the overgrown path to our favorite spot. We settled in, and I saw the wind ripple the water out toward the center of the lake.

"Son, one day I'm going to be rich and we are going to have a bass and a bream pond in our backyard. And we're going to wake up each morning and fish every day without having to go anywhere."

"When, Dad?" I asked, desperately.

"Soon, son," he said, with the confidence of a young man whose whole life was in front of him, his cigarette hanging from his mouth and an open beer between his legs.

I picked up a rock and threw it sidearm over the water, watching it skip three times as a flock of American coots scampered and flew away.

The cab was still waiting for me when I walked back to the road and stopped short of the car, looking back one last time.

"Everything all right?" he asked as I got in.

"Time to leave" is all I said.

17

The helicopter descended. I craned my neck upward as it came to a delicate rest on the UCLA rooftop. A man stepped out and shook my hand, and the helicopter blades tossed our hair in our faces.

"How's he doing?" I yelled to him over the sound.

"He's stable!" he screamed back.

Dad had always felt pain in his knees left over from his days of playing baseball. The bursitis in his right elbow flared up once or twice a month, and he had other small ailments, none of which he spoke of much. But this was different.

As he sat up on the couch at his home in Louisiana, reading his racing form, he must've felt a sudden numbness—a shortness of breath and throbbing in his hands—but something worse was happening to his feet. He hoped they had fallen asleep, but this wasn't a sleep pain. He labored to get his feet to the floor. As they swung over and touched the tile, he noticed that they had ballooned out to black-and-blue stumps. In a panic, he tried to stand, and then he lost consciousness.

He opened his eyes to the blurry blue-and-gray sky that moved above. Everything looks different when you're flat on your back. The oxygen mask pressed into his cheeks, his eyes watering from the sweat. He heard the sounds of the paramedics, but didn't understand what they were saying, and realized he had a needle in his arm and was rolling. He watched the blurry canopy of clouds slide past him as the pine trees swayed in the warm breeze. The sun soothed him for a moment, but was eclipsed by a huge black blade circling overhead. As he tried to lift his head, he found he was strapped down. The paramedic patted his arm to reassure him.

As his abdomen rose and fell arrhythmically, grasping at life, he heard the cacophony of the chopper and felt the stabbing in his lower body. He grunted in agony as they thrust him into the steel cage. Dad could see the paramedic's mouth moving, but he couldn't hear a word he was saying. The paramedics secured and tightened Dad's apparatus, and then one of them gave the thumbs-up sign to the pilot, who returned it.

As the chopper blasted everything around it with wind, Dad's head began to clear and his heart began to race as he overheard the word "Los Angeles." What a godforsaken, frightening place. It occurred to him that, depending upon what happened next, he might not be back.

As the helicopter lifted, Dad watched everything he knew disappear below him. The old antebellum mansion, Shadows on the Teche, whose white columns had housed cotton planters, slaves, courtly manners, and mint juleps in different times. The small house he grew up in on Duperier Avenue and, beside it, the old hospital where all of his children were born. Cooks Superette, the convenience store on Jane Street, where for twenty-five years he had bought his morning paper and coffee each day. The duck club Le Canard Mort on Pecan Island, where he sang "God Bless America" on mornings before a hunt with men he loved. The Freez-o drive-in on Center Street, near the old high school, where he ate chili dogs and shrimp po'boys with Mom on their early dates.

And as they flew over Spanish Lake, deeper memories surfaced of when he and his daddy shot ducks over early-morning sunrises,

before school, before limits, before game wardens, before conserva-
tion, before the Wildlife and Fisheries Department regulated the
killing.

He recalled his father's face at the light of dawn, against the
background of deeply hued sunrises. His black, horn-rimmed
glasses snug on his nose and his duck call lanyard hanging freely on
his chest. He remembered the nutria rats swimming through the
decoys, and the mullet fish jumping. He remembered taking target
practice on the blackbirds and getting instruction from his papa
when the ducks were slow.

He was six when he first sat in a blind on that lake with Hop,
and now he was sixty-four. As the helicopter pulled away from the
lake, he remembered it was once one of the finest hunting grounds
in the world—before it was drained, like much of his homeland.
Before coastal erosion, before oil and gas industrialization, before
progress destroyed many of the marshlands—before, when Louisiana was bigger, like him.

When the love and the money are gone, there are recrimina-
tions. Mom left Dad in 1999, long after they had spent most of the
money he'd saved. Mom bitterly judged him for having spent so
many days at the Evangeline Downs Racetrack, the offtrack betting parlor on the edge of town, and the La Fonda Mexican buffet.
Dad said she spent too much on nonsense, and that it took two to
tango—he wrote her a nasty note suggesting that she should get a
job instead of a lawyer. It all came to a head soon after he'd been
through rehab in Arizona for gambling and alcohol. It was a tough
program, and Dad came back changed, but it never stuck. By that
time, his health had started to slip away, too. Theirs had been a
forty-year union.

Like most of the Southern women of her generation, Mom

had little knowledge of Dad's business. According to her, they were supposed to have been partners, but in retrospect, she never did understand how the money was made, only that she needed it to live. She says she tried to participate in the conversation whenever he seemed stressed or quiet, but he wouldn't allow it. She said, when it was ending, that he never told the truth about much, and that the little lies became his life. But Dad was right, it does take two to tango.

Mom never talked to her father, C.B., about the divorce. The term "divorce" wasn't really in Paw's lexicon. He lived by the Ten Commandments, and when he made a commitment, he never wavered. Paw didn't have bad days or good days or bear markets or bull markets. Paw just lived and did what he had to do to provide for his family. C.B. died a few years after the divorce. Mom was crushed. And so was Dad, as C.B. had been the real rock in our family.

Over time, everyone in the family became increasingly concerned about the blockage in Dad's arteries and the poor condition of his feet. None of us quite realized how bad it had become. In the meantime, Bryan continued to rise to the top of deal making in Hollywood, and my ability, courage, and independence within the investing community grew.

Tutu had accepted life as a bachelor and was still chipping away in the horse racing business, even though the stands were now more sparsely populated, as consumer tastes had changed; the advent of online poker had taken a lot of leverage away from pari-mutuel betting. Still, he loved the ponies and all the people involved with them. This was a love that would never die.

Deb had a third child, Hunter, with another man, but this relationship didn't last either. She continued to walk her own path, and would often visit Mom, who by then lived alone and longed for companionship but enjoyed the love of her two youngest children still living so close. Hers was a life animated by family ties.

Back on the rooftop of the UCLA Medical Center, I studied the top of the building, mostly weathered by the elements but with the X still freshly painted in red. Dad's helicopter had met with a jet that carried him eighteen hundred miles, allowing him to connect with yet another chopper; now the dust and dirt kicked up on the rooftop as this second one descended.

Looking down, my father saw only asphalt, glass, steel, and cars; the lines in his face deepened.

I watched the pilot put the bird down smoothly and cut the engines. After I greeted my escort, a paramedic, he opened up the gate and we crouched toward the chopper. The door slid open, and there was Dad.

The paramedics nodded a greeting with that look of pity they so often wear. They extended the gurney, and I approached Dad on his left. The usual emergency gear was strapped to his face, his chest, and his arms. What wasn't so usual about any of this was his feet. His toenails were yellow, his toes swollen, and his feet and ankles were engorged and purple.

Our eyes met, and his lips tightened. I knew that he could see my pity. He tried to ease my fear with a wrinkled smile, but all I could see was what was hidden behind it, a truly enigmatic, paradoxical, supernatural thing covered in perishable flesh.

Today, he would lose his legs. I just hoped he wouldn't lose his life.

I walked next to the hospital bed as an intern and an on-call nurse wheeled Dad into the operating room at the UCLA Medical Center. We walked slowly, avoiding the life-saving equipment that lines the halls. A piece of tape was stuck to one of the wheels of the bed. I listened to it slap the floor rhythmically. I rested my hand on his arm, which was covered with liver spots and freckles, as he stared ahead. His hair was gone and his eyes were tired. Gone also were the wisecracks and jokes. I had not heard him say "I never had a bad day" in a very long time.

I tried to read the names that were written on the hospital doors with rub-away ink and white tape. Machines filled the hallways, which were lined with rooms full of patients succumbing to the great leveler, time. On every third or fourth door, a red sign cautioned "Do Not Enter." The machines tried to lend the dying and infirm a little more life. I smelled chlorine. Chlorine and death.

I heard ESPN blaring from one of the rooms, and I glanced in. An overweight woman with an expressionless face was reading a romance novel called *No Surrender*. She sat next to her husband, who labored through an oxygen mask. He was sweating profusely. His eyes were slits, and one of his legs, full of sores and veins, hung loosely over the side of the bed. My eyes met his. His toenails were yellow. I looked away.

The doctors walking the halls had names I couldn't pronounce—the progeny of cultures who still value service over wealth. Nurses walked in and out of rooms and down the halls, wearing green and turquoise scrubs, oblivious to me, to the man lying in this bed, and to the long downward spiral that had led us here.

I looked down at the white sheet that covered my pop and at his red, black, and purple feet. A nurse walked by with nice cleavage. I smiled. She didn't smile back.

Dad was not talking. He didn't blink. He stared ahead. I towered over him, holding on to the headboard. I could see dirt and dust on the lenses of his glasses. I could see the operating room—the point of no return—just ahead.

We arrived at the white doors. I noticed the walls inside were blue. The nurse picked up the phone on the wall and said "Harvey Lourd" into the receiver. The doors opened, and Dr. Diwaldi walked out to meet us in his scrubs. He shook my hand and turned to Dad with a concerned but relaxed expression.

"Mr. Lourd, how are you feeling?" I detected an accent, but wasn't sure of its origin.

"I'm ready. Go for it, Doc," Dad said without looking up. He played it cool, but I knew it was a lie. I tried to catch his flickering gaze, but he wouldn't let me—so I gave his arm a squeeze before looking at the doctor.

"Don't worry, he's going to be fine," Diwaldi said.

"Okay, I'll be in his room, waiting."

"Please, there is no need to do that. The operation will take three hours and then he'll sleep for twelve or fifteen after that. Go home or back to work. One of the nurses will call."

He had one hand on Dad's arm. I liked his bedside manner.

"Okay," I said, looking at my watch. It was eight a.m.

"You all right, Dad?" I asked.

"Yes, son," he said, still avoiding my gaze as he took off his glasses and handed them to me. "Make sure these don't get lost," he said, as if I were eight years old.

"Okay, Pop, I'll do that. I'll be here when you wake up." I could hear fear in his voice and in mine.

The doctor removed his hand from Dad's arm, grabbed the guardrail, and started to roll Dad away. Two nurses appeared in scrubs as the white doors closed in front of me.

I walked back to his room and set his glasses down on the crowded nightstand, then strode to the elevator. I pressed the button for the lobby and stood next to the long faces of the grieving and bereaved as we went down. I exited first, rudely, in front of some old ladies and an old man. I had to get out of there.

The sliding glass doors opened up to the large cement patio. I walked outside, squinting, and retrieved my sunglasses from my suit jacket pocket. The light is always the same in Los Angeles.

Men with intravenous tubes sticking out of their arms smoked cigarettes and flicked ashes on the stained cement. Family members stood around them, and not much was said. My car was parked in a doctor's spot, two hundred paces from the sitting area. There were "No Parking/Doctors Only" signs posted, but I'd parked there anyway.

I thought about leaving. A park bench next to a grassed-in area caught my eye, and I sat down. I didn't want to leave. I wanted to stay near him—as though my staying close could impact the outcome.

Eventually, however, I did go home, and the hours waned, slipping into dusk the way a memory slowly dissolves into nothing more than a feeling. Then, when I'd almost finally lapsed into sleep, I was at last allowed to go see him.

As I entered room 9130, my eyes immediately roving to the cylinder-like casts on my father's legs, within me there remained a disquiet about everything said and unsaid. I watched him breathe. The monitoring equipment next to his bed was calm, as was his sleeping face. He had a tube taped to his mouth, and he did not appear to be in pain. The curtains were still drawn. I opened them onto a new sun rising and wandered over to the nightstand to pick up his glasses, which were resting where I'd put them earlier. The frame was slightly bent and the lenses were scratched. I cleaned them off with my rooster-patterned tie.

I reached into his pants, pulled out his wallet, and looked through it. Inside was an old photograph of me with my siblings and Mom standing behind us. She looked about twenty-five. It choked me up, as I was not expecting to find that here. I wondered—if his luck had changed or he had gotten it together over the last decade or so— whether my parents would still be together now. The only other thing in his wallet was a ten-dollar betting slip from the Evangeline Downs Racetrack. It must have been a winning ticket. Why else would he have kept it?

"Blaine? Is that you?"

I quickly turned my head from the rising sun reflected in the glare of the office buildings on Wilshire Boulevard to find the surgeon.

"He's probably not going to wake up for a few more hours, but the surgery went great. Where are your brothers? Your dad was bragging about all you boys and your sister yesterday."

"Tutu and Deb are in Louisiana. Bryan is on his way back from New York. He'll be here soon." I turned, walked to him and looked him in the eye. "Doc, do you think he can be fitted for prosthetics?"

"It's a possibility, but really, it's up to him. Prosthetics in a case like this require a lot of effort."

"I'm sure we can find him good care in Lafayette," I said.

The doctor hesitated momentarily. "Blaine, maybe he hasn't spoken to you about this yet, but your dad told me last night that he doesn't want to go back to Louisiana."

"He said that?" I asked.

"Yes."

I looked at the doctor for a moment to see if he was kidding. "This guy right here?" I asked, pointing to my father, who lay unconscious in the bed.

"Yes"—he chuckled—"that guy right there."

After the doctor left the room, I sat down next to my father and tried to process this news. The only thing that seemed less likely than my father living without legs was my father living in Los Angeles. Could that be possible? Reflecting upon it in that moment, my answer was a resounding *no*. But that is, in fact, what happened.

I turned to stare at my father. I studied his supine body, his neck bent downward, his double chin on his shoulders, his false teeth on the bedside table, an oxygen mask on his face, tubes protruding from his arms—and, most shockingly, his legs gone below the knee. And as I took in the white-casted, gauze-taped cylinders that once were his legs, I felt myself ascending in rank, alone.

For the next eight years, Dad lived in a bedroom of Bryan's house. He never did learn to walk again; his muscles were too atrophied to ever make that journey to a fully upright position. Instead, he relied upon around-the-clock care provided by twin African American brothers from Inglewood, California.

It didn't happen all at once, but Dad finally began to see Bryan for who he was, and to be truly proud of him, recognizing the independence, courage, and drive that made him capable of pivoting, again and again, until the ground was as steady as a rock—an anvil—beneath him. Every day when Bryan got home, he would sit with Dad as he ate supper. Dad would be watching reruns of *The Rockford Files* or a Boston Red Sox game, or *Crime Stories*, but as Bryan walked in, he'd turn off the tube, put down his racing form, and eat and talk.

They'd talk about Bryan's business or about what they might cook for dinner that weekend—which would usually involve Dad supervising the making of some sort of Louisiana sauce: sauce piquant, gumbo, or shrimp stew, which was probably his favorite.

Sometimes they'd talk about relatives—some long since passed, and some more recently, like Nettie and Hop. Dad always got choked up when he talked about his mom. And when Hop died, a class of rigidity all its own dissolved back into the soil, leaving just the rest of us Lourd men. It didn't come easy, but even a man like my father could change. After they were done visiting, Bryan would always ask Dad if he needed anything. And Dad would always reply, "No, son. Thank you. I'm all set."

Harvey H. "Puffer" Lourd Jr. died on August 20, 2011. The whole family gathered for his memorial in a Main Street bar in New Iberia, and among many other people who loved him very much, I spoke as he was remembered. Everyone smiled and said he was one of a kind, and I smiled and pumped their hands, knowing better than anyone that this was true.

A couple of months after Dad passed, I flew back to see Mom, and went by to clean up Dad's old house. I cleaned off the coffee table that for years had doubled as his dinner table, toe-cleaning bench, medicine cabinet, and desk, and found dozens of empty prescription bottles: pain pills, blood thinners, vitamins, diabetes medications, and horse vitamins. I tossed out denture cream and four old steak knives wrapped in soiled paper towels that he'd stashed in the table drawer. I found a card holder housing all his old oil field contacts, and business cards from his last two jobs. There was a résumé filled with typos. I could feel the desperation in the flawed prose. Under the couch, I found the computer manual that he bought when he attended Vo-Tech, a vocational college, after his business failed and he had been through detox at Sierra Tucson.

Then I found books on gambling—*Picking Winners: A Horseplayer's Guide* and an unopened second edition of *Sharing Recovery*

Through Gamblers Anonymous, which must have been given to him by a pink-cloud-ridin' twelve-stepper. As I rummaged through his life, I must have thrown away ten thousand betting slips—the average bet eighteen dollars, some as high as five hundred. Looking at those slips, I realized that, after the oil-boom times, the offtrack betting parlor became his boardroom, his new seat of power.

We all hold what we have to. I've learned much about what to be and do, and what not to be and do, from a man who rode the crest and learned the difference between luck and grace the hard way. I've learned that the brand-new car or mower will always become the damned old car or mower, in the same way people sometimes become old friends not from a deepening of closeness over time but instead, by default, through the simple passing of time. And hardest of all, I've learned that we have nothing so important as the silence we keep with ourselves, and that the money we waste on what we love may, in the end, be the only wealth we do not squander, and that generosity is never wasted because nothing else endures, and it may be all we carry with us out the window.

I got up from the couch and walked over to the kitchen, washing my hands and looking out the window at a rolling stretch of overgrown grass much in need of a Poulan and a discerning eye atop an eight-horsepower mower. I studied the flow of the insects riding the warm, humid delta breeze, and then took in the clouds settling and resettling in endless formations high above. Then I turned, walked to the stacks of stuffed trash bags, and carried to the outside bin a lifetime of old tax returns, bets, and paperwork.

As I walked back into his bedroom, something caught my eye in his half-opened closet, and I approached it and looked inside. There hung the clothes I'd always remembered him in, the clothes that defined my father—the houndstooth all-in-one, his camouflage overalls, and his Red Wing steel-toe work boots. Hanging on a hook, partly covered with some bad ties, was his old belt, the buckle now a bit tarnished, the word "Coonass" hammered across the back. And there on the floor next to a pair of worn-out alligator boots was a postcard that must have fallen out of a shoe box of old letters and photographs he kept on the top shelf.

I picked up the card and turned it over in my hands. It was an old postcard I'd sent Dad after Mom divorced him. On the back I'd written, "Things have a way of settling where they are supposed to. Hopefully, your new life will steal the great parts of you back from the past and bring them into the future." I smiled faintly, thinking that still held true for me, now. The front of the card had a picture of an older, skilled man blowing into a duck call atop a clear lake at what looked like dawn—the water dark and perfectly still.

There's a chance my dad kept this card because what I'd written had made him feel better, or inspired him in some way. But I doubt it. I'm pretty sure he just liked looking at the picture—imagining the two of us out there on a lake like that at that hour in a duck blind, waiting. "Get ready, son," he would instruct as the birds circled overhead. And then his voice would soften to a whisper, "Let them pass one more time," and I'd feel that sharp tug of anticipation. We would raise our guns to our shoulders, fix our eyes down the barrels, and aim into the bright Louisiana morning.

ACKNOWLEDGMENTS

First, I'd like to thank Richard Morris, an agent and a friend who never wavered in his dedication to this story and to me.

Sherion B. Lourd, Mom, who reminded all of us from the bayou, whenever we needed to hear it, that "we had what it takes."

To my brothers and sister, who have my heart and who blessed this project from the moment I started it, with no fear.

This book was birthed on a boat in the Yucatán Peninsula, while fishing with my brother-in-law, James R. "Bubba" Moffett Jr. We had a stingy captain who was more worried about gas than fish. He dragged the same dead reef for six hours before I retired to the cabin to write the Mexico chapter. Thank you, Bubba, for sharing boats and blinds with me.

There were several important women involved at each iteration of this manuscript. The first is Laurie Ann Post, a writer, a filmmaker, a seeker, and the woman who gave me the friendship, confidence, and support to finish the first draft of this book.

Joanie Wread. A great friend and a truly gifted editor, who has read and reread every word written in every chapter of this book dozens of times. A survivor, a creator, a mother, an inspiration to me, without whose dedication this project would have never been completed.

Alison Callahan, my editor at Gallery, who, although late to the project, helped me to see this story in an entirely new light.

Lastly, I'd like to thank my team at LourdMurray for accepting both parts of me—pensive, grouchy writer and pensive, grouchy money manager—and for living the truth in an industry that likes to hide it.